Key Thinkers of the English, Scottish and American Enlightenments

Sabrina P. Ramet · Torbjørn L. Knutsen

Key Thinkers of the English, Scottish and American Enlightenments

From Locke to Madison

Sabrina P. Ramet
Department of Sociology & Political
Science
NTNU
Trondheim, Norway

Torbjørn L. Knutsen
Department of Sociology & Political
Science
NTNU
Trondheim, Norway

ISBN 978-3-031-62453-7   ISBN 978-3-031-62454-4   (eBook)
https://doi.org/10.1007/978-3-031-62454-4

Cover illustration: © Harvey Loake

This Palgrave Macmillan imprint is published by the registered company Springer Nature
Switzerland AG
The registered company address is: Gewerbestrasse 11, 6330 Cham, Switzerland

If disposing of this product, please recycle the paper.

In memory of
Benedictus de Spinoza (1632–1677)

PREFACE

We undertook work on this volume in the realization that, although many fine volumes have been published dealing with the Enlightenment as a whole,[1] as well as with the English Enlightenment thinkers (John Locke, Algernon Sidney), Scottish Enlightenment thinkers (above all David Hume and Adam Smith), and American Enlightenment thinkers (Thomas Jefferson, James Madison, Thomas Paine) separately, to the best of our knowledge there has been no volume published in English bringing the English, Scottish, and American Enlightenment thinkers together in one volume. This is so despite the fact that several scholars writing about Jefferson and Madison have noted how much the Americans were influenced by the writings of Locke, Sidney, Hume, and the French jurist and philosopher Baron de Montesquieu, as well as by the pre-Enlightenment thinker Thomas Hobbes. Mary Wollstonecraft, an English radical, read the works of Locke, Hume, Immanuel Kant, and Jean-Jacques Rousseau, among others, but bridled against Rousseau's championing of gender inequality.

---

[1] See, for example: Anthony Pagden, *The Enlightenment: And why it still matters* (Oxford: Oxford University Press, 2015); *Ritchie Robertson, The Enlightenment: The Pursuit of Happiness 1680–1790* (Harmondsworth: Penguin, 2022); John Robertson, *The Enlightenment: A Very Short Introduction* (Oxford: Oxford University Press, 2015); and Roy Porter, *Enlightenment: Britain and the Creation of the Modern World* (Harmondsworth: Penguin, 2001).

Whether one thinks of Locke or Sidney in England or Jefferson, Madison, or Paine in the New World, the major Enlightenment thinkers were all motivated by *political* considerations ranging from opposition to royal absolutism to demands for religious toleration to their commitment to the principles, as stated in the American Declaration of Independence, that "all men are created equal" and enjoy "certain unalienable rights [including]...Life, Liberty and the Pursuit of Happiness"—or, as John Locke had put it, "Life, Liberty, and Property." In the British colonies in the New World, soon to be established as the United States, Jefferson, Madison, and Paine were all well versed in the Enlightenment writings.

The *central themes* of the Anglo-American Enlightenment, which emerge in all of the chapters included in this volume, are *Reason, Morality, Liberty (or Freedom), and Rights* (the last of these embracing also *Equality)*—explicitly developed in the conclusion. *Secondary themes,* highlighted in the introduction and in Chapter 3, are respectively Progress (in the introduction) and "the existence of a unifying moral force" and the impact of Newtonian physics on how these thinkers may be thought to have approached politics (in Chapter 3). Locke and Sidney were demanding change and wanted to see a greater role for parliament; Jefferson and Madison found themselves as architects of political change, with Jefferson in particular, in some places, paraphrasing the words of Locke.

We are grateful to Ambra Finotello, our commissioning editor at Palgrave Macmillan, for commissioning feedback from two well-qualified scholars and to those scholars for their detailed and most helpful suggestions.

Trondheim, Norway
January 2024

Sabrina P. Ramet
Torbjørn L. Knutsen

CONTENTS

ABOUT THE AUTHORS

Sabrina P. Ramet is a Professor Emerita at the Norwegian University of Science & Technology (NTNU). She earned her Ph.D. in Political Science at UCLA in 1981. She is the author of 16 scholarly monographs, including *Alternatives to Democracy in Twentieth-Century Europe: Collectivist Visions of Modernity* (Central European University Press, 2019) and *East Central Europe and Communism: Politics, Culture, and Society, 1943-1991* (Routledge, 2023), and co-author (with Lavinia Stan) of *East Central Europe since 1989: Politics, Culture, and Society* (Routledge, in production). She is also the editor or co-editor of 40 books, including *Central and Southeast European Politics since 1989*, 2nd ed. (Cambridge University Press, 2019). Her previous work in political philosophy includes articles on Martin Heidegger (in *Religion Compass*, Vol. 6, no. 9, 2012), Jean Bodin (in *Politics and Religion/Politikologija religije*, Vol. XIII, Issue 1, 2019), Benedictus de Spinoza (in *Teorija in praksa*, Vol. 60, no. 2, 2023), and John Rawls and Robert Nozick (in *Teorija in praksa*, Vol. 61, no. 1 (2024). She and Torbjørn Knutsen are co-authors of *German Moral and Political Philosophy, 1785–1908: A concise introduction* (New Academia Publishing, 2023).

Torbjørn L. Knutsen is a Professor Emeritus at the Norwegian University of Science & Technology (NTNU) and at the Norwegian Air Force Academy. He earned his Ph.D. in Political Science at the University of

Denver in 1986. His books include *A History of International Relations Theory,* 3rd ed. (University of Manchester Press, 2016), *Norsk utenrikspolitisk idéhistorie 1890–1940,* co-authored with Halvard Leira and Iver B. Neumann (Universitetsforlaget, 2016), *Ways of Knowing: Competing Methodologies in Social and Political Research,* 3rd ed., co-authored with Jonathon W. Moses (Palgrave Macmillan, 2019), *Tenke og skrive i samfunnsvitenskapene,* co-authored with Tormod Heier (Fagbokforlaget, 2021), *German Moral and Political Philosophy, 1785–1908: A concise introduction,* co-authored with Sabrina P. Ramet (New Academia Publishing, 2023), and *The Rise and Fall of Terrorism* (Universitetsforlaget, 2024). His previous work in political philosophy includes an article on Jean-Jacques Rousseau (in *Journal of Peace Research,* Vol. 31, no. 3, 1994) and a chapter on Niccolò Machiavelli (in *Politisk filosofi: Fra Platon til Hannah Arendt* (Pax Forlag, 2013).

CHAPTER 1

Introduction: The Seeds of Enlightenment

Torbjørn L. Knutsen

Abstract This chapter locates the seeds of the Enlightenment among the humanist authors of the Renaissance. Tracing their germination through the Reformation, it notes that they found the most fertile conditions in countries in Western Europe and sprouted most readily there, whereas they fell on more stony ground in countries further east and south. During the seventeenth century, the first buds of Enlightenment thought burst open in countries along the North Atlantic rim: in the Netherlands, England, Scotland, and along the eastern coastline of North America. Here Enlightenment ideas supported the establishment of a republic devoted to the ideas that human beings as endowed with Reason and with Rights—including the Right to life, liberty, and property—and the idea that human History describes a progressive evolution of knowledge, freedom, and happiness.

Keywords Renaissance · Reason · Rights · Thirty Years' War · Glorious Revolution · English Civil War · Age of Discovery · Religious strife · Scientific progress

The Enlightenment goes by many names—the Age of Reason, the Age of Revolution, the Age of Cosmopolitanism .... Regardless of name, it

© The Author(s), under exclusive license to Springer Nature
Switzerland AG 2024
S. P. Ramet and T. L. Knutsen, *Key Thinkers of the English, Scottish and American Enlightenments*,
https://doi.org/10.1007/978-3-031-62454-4_1

commonly refers to a period from the mid-seventeenth century to the end of the eighteenth, in which an intellectual movement ignited the flame of reason, liberty, and progress.

It is rarely called the Age of Upheaval, even though it was a time of great turbulence. It introduced new ideas—for example, the notion that "all men are created equal" and endowed with "unalienable Rights." These ideas had revolutionary effects. They dismissed old arguments of royal absolutism and divine right and replaced them with ideals of popular sovereignty and republican government. This triggered ferocious opposition. The Enlightenment, then, was an age of struggle, social upheaval, and political conflict. The new ideas may be seen already during Thirty Years War (1618–1648). They became clearly visible during England's Glorious Revolution (1688–1689). And they reached a climax in the American and French Revolutions during the final quarter of the eighteenth century.

What kinds of ideas were these? What were the key concepts that generated the Enlightenment? And where did they come from? A full answer to these questions leads us far back in Western history. Some ideas are found in the discussions about human Reason in the city-states of Renaissance Italy; others orbit the concept of Rights which emerged from the English Civil War; still other ideas flow from the discussions of Progress which were conducted in the seafaring nations along the North Atlantic rim and produced new philosophies of History during the first half of the eighteenth century.

These Enlightenment ideas are readily found in late eighteenth-century discussions. For example, in the revolutionary writings of Thomas Paine—who drew inspiration from past writers like Milton, Priestley, and Price. They can be seen in the texts of Thomas Jefferson, who drew on the theories of Sidney, Locke, and Hume. And in the texts of James Madison, who was inspired by Machiavelli's *Discourses* and Montesquieu's *Spirit of the Laws*. The central themes of the Anglo-American Enlightenment—Reason, Rights, and Progress—stem from fifteenth- and sixteenth-century seeds that germinated and evolved during the seventeenth century and sprang into bloom during the eighteenth.

1.1 THE SEEDS AND THE AGE OF REASON

This chapter does not see the "Age of Reason" and the "Enlightenment" as synonymous terms. Rather, the Age of Reason is seen as the longer, more encompassing period; it has its roots in the Renaissance. Its origins are indicated by new ways in which Renaissance scholars described Nature. Whereas ancient and medieval scholars had perceived human beings as part of Nature, Renaissance thinkers began to separate the two. Human beings are part of Nature, but they are uniquely equipped with speech, Reason, and independent Will. And human societies are not part of Nature. They are not ruled by fortune or God, but by artifacts organized by powerful men with Reason and free Will.

This argument is expressed by Renaissance thinker Niccolò Machiavelli, who claimed that about half of human actions are results of man's own will and reason—the remaining half is dictated by fortune.[1] This idea would, as the Age of Reason unfolded, eventually produce the Enlightenment vision that by applying Will and Reason, and by accumulating and systematizing knowledge, humans could master Nature and engineer good societies marked by justice, peace, and plenty.

As the Age Reason unfolded, the new view of Nature brought forth three clusters of ideas. These concerned Reason, Rights, and Progress. Their consequences were most readily felt in societies along the northwestern rim of Europe's Atlantic coast.

The Great Discoveries of Nature

The rise of the Age of Reason marked the fading out of the medieval civilization. It is hard to pinpoint its exact beginning, although the Oration on the Dignity of Man (1486) by Giovanni Pico della Mirandola (1463–1494) is often taken as marking the symbolic start of the Renaissance. Suffice it to say, that it took time, that it involved replacing old doctrines with new, secular knowledge, and that the transition began seamlessly during the Renaissance and the Age of Discovery. The most famous discoveries of the Renaissance resulted from voyages and sightings that greatly expanded human knowledge about the geography of the earth. But they also included discoveries in time: the findings of antique texts which greatly enriched the knowledge of the historical past. These discoveries went hand in hand with a secular outlook, a systematic and empirical approach that was anchored in a new faith in human Reason and in the idea of human mastery over Nature.

The long voyages and the discoveries in space were unique to the Renaissance. The discoveries in time, however, were really rediscoveries— the resurrection of ideas and arguments rescued from a distant past. They included the rediscoveries of texts by Plato and Thucydides. Although they had been written in an ancient world, the descriptions of life in ancient city-states were recognized by urban readers in Renaissance Italy. The texts included discussions of architecture, farming, medicine, and other practical topics that provided new and useful knowledge. And they were attended by an implication that rocked traditional scholarship: All this new knowledge, which more practical, more useful, and more empirically correct than anything the Church could offer, was older than Christ. It was produced by an ancient civilization that existed long before Christendom and the Church.

New knowledge about the past and about the geography of the present led to the greatest discovery of all: of Man. It was developed by the movement of humanist scholars who evolved outside the age-old educational monopoly of the Church. This movement was sponsored by merchants, tradesmen, and other secular actors. They discovered logical inconsistencies in the teachings of the Church. They challenged the accuracy of Church wisdom. And they asked why biblical accounts neglected to mention the high civilization of ancient Greece or the existence of newly discovered lands. These humanist activities affected an early shift from medieval scholarship to a new reliance on empirical observation and experiment.

The new knowledge was reflected in new maps. These were drawn by sailors who, after Columbus, set out on long expeditions to unknown regions of the earth and who wrote about what they saw. These expeditions reflect a change in human attitudes to Nature. Before Columbus (1451–1506), sailors were loath to let go of the sight of land. Their ships tended to scurry along the coastlines, hugging known and safe shores. After Columbus, this quickly changed. Within a generation, the oceans no longer represented a barrier to maritime ventures. The blue horizon no longer represented the limit for safe navigation; instead, it represented a challenge, an invitation to new knowledge, and opportunities for wealth and fame.

Humanist scholars of the Renaissance produced new maps of the earth, new charts of the heavens, and new anatomical studies of the human body.

These novelties challenged traditional ways of perceiving the world, the universe, Man, and society. That meant that they challenged the Church. During the sixteenth century, intellectuals including Lorenzo Valla (ca 1406–1457), Desiderius Erasmus (1466–1536), and Martin Luther (1483–1546) challenged established Church doctrines with a new spirit of inquiry, critical thinking, and an individualist perspective of human nature.

On Conflict, War, and the Division Between East and West

The Age of Reason was an age of religious conflict, political tension, and struggles for power. A major source of tension was the rise of a new kind of ruler: Powerful monarchs who centralized and concentrated their power. They did this at the expense of local lords who resisted the new monarchs' state-building efforts with armed rebellions. As a result, the Age of Reason was a period of European civil wars. And it was intensified by religious strife.

England offers a famous example. Here state-building and religious reform reenforced each other during the reign of Henry VIII Tudor (1491–1547). The king broke with the pope, confiscated Church properties, and used it to reorganize the power structure of the land and create a new, national Church. Other kings soon followed his example. In northern Europe, several kings converted to Protestantism and appointed themselves heads of new, national churches. The new clergy would, in turn, use their normative authority to legitimize the military might and the economic fortunes of the Kings.

Religious strife was one of the drivers of the civil wars that marked the age. But it also affected the rivalry among the new monarchs who sought to consolidate their central power at home and expand it abroad. Others were interstate wars, fought by kings who competed for territory and honor. The kings would regularly invoke religion to justify their causes. During the Age of Reason, then, wars—whether they were civil wars of interstate wars—would have a religious aspect to them, regularly reflecting conflicting interpretations of the Christian scriptures.

The first half of the seventeenth century was kept in a fever of such wars, and they all affected some change in Europe's political landscape. The French Wars of Religion (1562–1598) weakened France. The Thirty Years' War (1618–1648)—a complex tangle of civil conflicts and interstate rivalries—weakened Central Europe. It also weakened religious authority and stimulated secular efforts to identify the moral and organizational preconditions for order and peace.[2] States that escaped these wars would experience a relative rise in power. The Netherlands and England, for example, rose to preeminence during these wars, although both were consumed by serious troubles of their own. The Netherlands was fractured by religious strife. England suffered a chain of political instability which erupted in vicious civil war (1642–1652) between King and Parliament. During the course of this war, Parliament invoked arguments that medieval barons had established to limit the power of the king and formulated a doctrine of citizens' rights.

On Communication: The Republic of Letters and the Public Sphere

The seventeenth-century wars divided Europe. The eastern parts of Europe remained a congeries of imperial states ruled by great landowners and based on agricultural economies. Here, ideas of Reason and Rights fell on stony ground. In the West, including Poland, however, the seeds of the Enlightenment germinated and struck roots. Here "new monarchies" built sovereign states with expanding economies fueled by commerce.

The Netherlands and England conducted expansionist foreign policies characterized by an expansion of long-distance trade and colonialism. This, in turn, gave rise to a new, wealthy, mercantile bourgeoisie in major port cities. Its members tended to view traditional institutions of Church and King as impediments to their mercantile activities. They favored ideas of freedom—individual freedom at home and free trade abroad. Their ideas were carried wide and far by new means of communication—notably by ships.

This expansion was the product of many innovations, first of all, by new ship designs and new instruments of navigation, but also, by more efficient printing presses and new, cheaper types of paper. This lowered the cost of books, journals, magazines, and newssheets. The expansion of shipping improved communication. New postal services allowed scholars to exchange letters and texts and, over time, provide a network of correspondence that transcended national boundaries.

Letters have existed since ancient times—early Christian missionaries (such as Paul) had written letters to Christian congregations. But during the seventeenth century, letter-writing expanded and reached a different scale altogether. Letters were used to send greetings and readings, to practice polemical writing, and to exchange ideas with like-minded others.

During the Age of Reason there evolved in Europe and North America a self-proclaimed network or community of scholars—a *"Res Publica Litterarum"* or "republic of letters."

This network of ideational exchanges among intellectuals grew denser as time progressed. And it is worth recalling that ideas of the age were not confined to an intellectual elite. The new perspectives and the attitudes they carried permeated society. They affected many domains of human endeavor—philosophy, economy, politics, religion, and arts—leaving indelible marks on society in its entirety.

But they altered some societies more than others. Their impact was small in societies where landowning elites cleaved to traditions upheld by an orthodox Church and where censorship was legitimized by religious faith. The greatest impact occurred in the open seafaring trading states that evolved along the North Atlantic rim. Here new ideas and attitudes swept into public spaces. Pubs, clubs, coffeehouses, and salons evolved and provided basic building blocks for the institution which supported the Enlightenment in a major way: The "public sphere."

Coffeehouses, which emerged in the busy ports of colonial powers—like Amsterdam and London—became popular meeting places for discussions and information. Entrepreneurial proprietors would hire writers to post or sell sheets of shipping news. As these were published more regularly and included additional information, they evolved into newspapers. Coffeehouses also served as venues for sailors seeking work, skippers seeking freights, sellers seeking customers, and agents who offered to introduce them all to one another. Lloyds of London was established by Edward Lloyd at his coffeehouse in 1688.

Such meeting places proliferated in the maritime cities of the West. During the seventeenth century there emerged stock exchanges, libraries, and social clubs which added to the dynamism of the public sphere. Reading clubs sprang up, where people would pool their cash, buy books, read, discuss, and store the books in a club library. Of particular significance were the scientific societies. The Royal Society of London and the French Academy of Sciences had both begun as social clubs, but by the mid-1660s they had evolved into public bodies, housed in a large building, and financially supported by monarchs. The societies held regular meetings, kept careful records, printed minutes and reports, and published them regularly in scientific journals.

Newton, Locke, and the Publicists

Many Society publications concerned pedestrian topics from everyday life. Some of them yielded insights of practical importance. A few triggered discussions of great scientific consequence. One of the most momentous discussions followed a 1687 presentation in the Royal Society, where Isaac Newton described the laws that governed the orbits of the planets. His *Philosophiae Naturalis Principia Mathematica* was printed and published under the Royal Society's seal. It triggered discussions far outside of the Society, England, and natural Philosophy.

John Locke was deeply impressed by Newton's work and sought to apply his method to his own study of politics.[3] Voltaire, who lived in the Netherlands during the 1720s and met many of the leading lights of Dutch and English society, was also impressed by Newton—and by Locke, by England's constitutional monarchy, and by the open and free discussions that marked England's public sphere. He marveled at its many different journals and magazines. Among them were Richard Steele's and Joseph Addison's *Tatler* and *Spectator*, Samuel Johnson's *Rambler* and *Idler*, Jonathan Swift's *Intelligencer*, Oliver Goldsmith's *Citizen of the World*, and others.

Along with such publications "publicists" emerged. Some were editors and "journalists" (such as Steele and Addison). Others were freelancers. But they all wrote for an expanding market. It is worth lingering on this point, first, because some publicists wrote long pieces of fiction and helped develop a novel kind of text—like Margareth Cavendish, Aphra Behn, Daniel Defoe, and Samuel Richardson.[4]

Second, it should be noted that some publicists had an immense effect on Enlightenment thought. Since they wrote for the market, they learnt to express themselves in ways that attracted the customers' attention. They used their wit to write comedies and satires. But also—and this is most relevant in this connection—their ironic texts were often written at the expense of politicians. They offered criticisms of governments, laws, and social conditions.[5] And they were quite aware of two things: That in order to be read, you first had to attract attention; consequently, to grab readers' attention, it was useful to develop radical arguments. Also, as they lived by their pen, they knew that their livelihood depended not only on their own quick wit and literary talents, but also on the continued existence of the public sphere. They had, in other words, an interest in defending freedom of expression.

If the intellectual life of Age of Reason was defined by the humanists, the Enlightenment was shaped by the publicists. Their defense of freedom was built into the Enlightenment from the outset. It lies at the heart of a key idea of the Enlightenment Age: that individual freedom is a Right.

1.2   The Enlightenment

When did the Enlightenment begin? During the final quarter of the seventeenth century is a reasonable assessment. It evolved slowly and its maturation is hard to map with precision. Also, as the Age of Reason evolved, institutions of previous ages did not disappear. Thus, the Age of Enlightenment is also the Age of the Old Regime. The Church, monarchy, heredity, status, and superstition held sway throughout the eighteenth century.[6] Yet, during the final decades of the seventeenth century, the contours of the Enlightenment came more clearly into view, e.g., in the writings of Spinoza, Sidney, and Locke.

What kind of contours were they? What were the views and ideas that grew during the Age of Reason and evolved into the characteristic attributes of the Enlightenment? These, too, are difficult questions to answer, because the Enlightenment was not the same in all countries. In the fog belt associated with the English Channel, Enlightenment attitudes emerged early—as exemplified by Dutch pioneers such as Simon Stevin, by thinkers who spent time in the Netherlands (René Descartes and Thomas Hobbes) and English luminaries such as Francis Bacon and Isaac Newton.

It is useful to distinguish between the Dutch/British Enlightenment with its empiricist orientation, and that of France, which had a more rationalist and analytic bent. However, all include four clusters of ideas. The two first ideas, Nature and Reason have been mentioned already. The next two, Rights and Progress, have been alluded to but will be more fully explored below.

Nature

Classical authors generally held nature to be wild and unpredictable; they saw human beings as part of nature. Medieval authors held a similar outlook but argued that Nature (with Man included) was created by God—and that God sometimes moved in mysterious and unpredictable ways. Renaissance scholars developed a different view. They separated humans from Nature. They held a view of humankind as creatures with Reason and independent Will. They viewed society as made and maintained by strong and determined leaders. And they developed the notion that humanity could, through Reason, Will, and labor, control Nature—domesticate it, so to speak, and make it obey rational regulation.

Machiavelli (1469–1527) provides an early example of this attitude. For him human behavior is not determined by God; it is the result of Reason, will, and power. States are not natural or divinely inspired (as the classical and medieval authors argued), but made and maintained by strong leaders. Fortune may fill rivers, cause them to overrun their banks, flood fields, uproot trees, raze buildings, and cause people to flee their homes. However, a wise ruler will develop distinct faculties and skills of leadership (*virtú*) to tackle such events. He will organize citizens and make them dig canals and erect defenses in fair weather so that fields and homes are spared when future floods occur.

As the Age of Reason progressed, attitudes toward Nature and Reason evolved. This is indicated by the changes that took place between early seventeenth-century authors such as Hugo Grotius and Thomas Hobbes, and later authors such as John Locke. Grotius argued that if humans were perfectly free, they would live without any authority. There would be no law to constrain their actions. They would obey no one. They would be "natural men" and live in a "state of nature." Such a state of nature would by definition be a state of lawlessness.[7]

Thomas Hobbes pursued this notion and described this state of natural liberty as chaotic and conflictual. He had England's horrible civil war in mind, when he described the state of nature as a state of "perpetuall war of all against all," in which human life is "nasty, brutish and short."

This view of a chaotic state of nature changed after the end of the destructive mid-century wars. John Locke did not describe the state of nature as a condition of violent lawlessness when he wrote toward the end of the 1680s. He described it as governed by Reason and the "law of Nature." Francis Hutchinson elaborated on Locke's view and argued that from Reason flowed a human sense of morality—an innate ability to distinguish between good and bad, just and unjust. For Hutcheson, this "moral sense" was no less real than the physical senses of sight, smell, touch, taste, and hearing.[8]

By that time, scholars were developing modern scientific methods. They steadily increased their knowledge about Nature and society. They also parted ways with the field of theology and developed two secular fields of learning: One field explored Nature (and was called "Natural Philosophy"). The other explored the social behavior of humans (and was designated "Moral Philosophy"). A university chair of Moral Philosophy was established at the University of Glasgow in 1727. Its first occupant, Gershom Carmichael, was succeeded by Francis Hutcheson. He divided the field of Moral Philosophy into four components: ethics, law, politics, and economics.[9]

At this point, the Enlightenment view of Nature was coming more clearly into view. Nature was no longer seen as unpredictable and wild; it obeyed universal laws. Natural philosophers like Galileo and Newton argued that humans could discover these laws by the systematic use of Reason. They demonstrated this by describing the movements of planets in the sky in the language of mathematics. By virtue of such laws, humans could predict storms and floods, build defenses against them, and make themselves masters of Nature.

Moral philosophers argued that human beings are not only rational, but also equal: That Reason is the same for everyone. And that when individuals think deeply about basic questions concerning justice and order, they will all use the same Reason and tend to come up with the same answers. Regardless of time and place. By systematic use of human Reason, humans can construct "universal" or "natural" moral norms.

Reason

The second great cluster of Enlightenment ideas, Reason, is closely related to the first. For Reason, properly working, would enable human beings to discover Nature—including the natural laws and norms that govern human interaction.

Reason involves disciplined thought. But it was more than the rules of logic established by ancient philosophers like Aristotle. For René Descartes (1595–1650), for example—who was born in France but settled in Holland—humans were more than "rational animals" and human Reason more than just logic and calculation. Reason is "thinking." It involves man's ability to observe and to critically evaluate the world and assess his own place in it.[10]

Thomas Hobbes (1588–1679), who spent the 1630s in France and Holland, was of a similar mind. He held that Reason is more than just "addition and subtraction." But he parted ways with Descartes' claim that the road to truth passes through thinking alone. Hobbes protested

Descartes' idea of innate knowledge. Instead, he held that the human mind must receive impressions from the material world. They must observe the world through their senses and then store the observations in the mind. Reason is, of course, indispensable, Hobbes maintained. However, Reason must work with "sense perception and memory" to produce true knowledge.[11]

In the late eighteenth century, John Locke seized upon Hobbes' discussion of "sense and memory" and developed it further. In his massive *Essay Concerning Understanding* (1689) Locke rejected Descartes' notion of innate ideas, like Hobbes had done before him, and emphasized observation and *sense* impressions as the exclusive source of knowledge. This essay, more than any other single text, provided the epistemological foundation for the Enlightenment's view of Reason. Locke not only rejected Descartes' view of innate ideas, but also drew implications which caused shockwaves to ripple through the community of traditional philosophers. He pointed out, for example, that Descartes' philosophy of knowledge presupposed a merciful God and divine revelation. But since divine revelation involves innate ideas, he continued, it cannot be considered a trustworthy source of knowledge. All knowledge, Locke insisted, is derived from perceptions of sense. These leave impressions upon the human mind in the form of memories.

Locke's idea, that the human mind is a blank slate from birth—a *tabula rasa*—on which experience inscribes a content, became the basis for the Enlightenment's philosophy of knowledge. It provided three pillars which supported a distinct political philosophy. The first flowed explicitly from the conditions under which Reason could be realized. The second was, more implicitly, related to relations between human individuals and the society in which they lived—between the inner mind which receives sense impressions and stores them memory, and the outer society from which these impressions originate.[12] These two pillars are discussed more closely in the next section, where they will be joined by a third pillar, which is drawn from Locke's philosophy of knowledge: the plea for a secular state. Since Locke's philosophy of knowledge sees divine revelation as untrustworthy, it cannot serve as a legitimate basis for a state.[13] Reason, however, can serve as such a basis, especially when combined with a claim of human equality: Together they will engender a doctrine of natural and universal Rights, which provides the legitimate basis for a state. The prime purpose of a state is not to save souls, but to protect and maintain humanity's natural Rights—primary among which are the individual Right to life, liberty, and property.

Rights

Thomas Hobbes (1588–1679) sowed the seed of the Enlightenment understanding of Rights. His book *Leviathan* begins by acknowledging that humans are creatures of Reason. But that in order to exercise Reason, humans must be free—i.e., they must be under no mortal threat or obligation to other persons. This introduces a conundrum: if all people were free, nobody would obey rules or laws. Society would be a lawless chaos. Is it possible, Hobbes asked, for people to be free without plunging society into disorder and chaos? Can human beings obey norms and rules and still be free? As Hobbes tackled these questions, he opened the door to an important Enlightenment argument: He formulated an answer in terms of the concept of Rights.

All humans are born free, Hobbes begins; they are all born with natural Rights to everything. However, if they all insist on exercising that natural Right, the result would be a chaotic "war of all against all." But humans are equal and rational. Therefore, they will understand that if everyone enjoys full individual freedom, they will create a social condition that is so violent and chaotic that no one can enjoy the fruits of this freedom. Therefore, for freedom to be practically meaningful, people must agree to give up the idea that they have a natural Right to everything. They must surrender their natural Right to everything, and invest this Right in a single, sovereign person—who then becomes all-powerful. They must pledge to obey this Sovereign. In turn, the Sovereign must promise to protect the most basic Rights of every citizen. These Rights are not only basic, but they are also universal, fundamental, inalienable, and natural products of Reason.

This reciprocal promise—in which all citizens agree to obey the Sovereign, and the Sovereign agrees to protect citizens' Rights—is a necessary condition for social order. It is the "Social Contract" upon which an orderly society is founded. And in this orderly society all citizens can live peacefully. Here, they can freely search for true knowledge and, through thinking and systematic doubt, realize their humanity.

Enlightenment thinkers balked at Hobbes' *Leviathan*. They rejected his idea that the only way to create order and peace was by pooling sovereignty and investing it in an all-powerful ruler. They opposed such absolutism. Yet, they accepted most of Hobbes' premises: Benedictus de Spinoza (1632–1677), Algernon Sidney (1623–1683), John Locke (1632–1704), and others accepted notions of basic Rights, a state of nature, a social contract, and a limited function of government. However, they based their arguments on different ideas about human nature. They differed from Hobbes in their views of Rights, Reason, and human relations. Consequently, they developed different ideas about human society and human conduct.

John Locke included (like Hobbes) Life and Liberty among humankind's natural Right. But he elaborated on Hobbes' discussion of the social preconditions for Life and Liberty and added Property as a third natural Right.[14] In addition, he developed an explanation for how Property is created (it is created through labor) as well as an account of the conditions under which Property can be justly acquired.[15] These two additions—the formulation of natural Rights as Life. Liberty, and Property, together with the labor theory of property—are among Locke's most important contributions to the Moral Philosophy of the Enlightenment.

A third contribution is more subtle. It flows from Locke's philosophy of knowledge and concerns the relation between the human mind and society[16]: Since all knowledge that exists in the human mind originates as sense impressions and that these are stored as memory, then whoever can control those basic sense impressions and can affect the human memory, can also shape the content of the human mind. This idea gave rise to an optimistic idea which became central in Enlightenment thought: That education can form the character of the individual.

Reason is disciplined thought. It is common sense but sharpened and made subtler by education—by training in both Natural and Moral Philosophy. By teaching people elementary skills, exposing them to good experiences, and applying them to moral questions, it would be possible to create a good society. The right education can form good individuals. Good individuals are allowed freedom to develop Reason and realize their potential of becoming a thinking, truly human, beings. This, in turn, will enhance social diversity, stimulate the steady creation of new knowledge, and steadily improve society.[17] In short, by education from early infancy on, it is possible to create societies marked by self-sustaining order, peace, and happiness.[18] This idea ties in with the final cluster of Enlightenment ideas, that of Progress.

Progress

Progress involves a linear view of history. It was adumbrated by Renaissance authors, such as Machiavelli. One of the first political thinkers to view human affairs in secular terms, free from supernatural and providential influences, Machiavelli argued that history and society are driven not by a divine plan, but by human beings who act according to Reason, Will, and self-interest. A systematic observer can identify regularities and patterns in human behavior, argued Machiavelli. His short book *The Prince*, shows how a ruler can rely on knowledge about such regularities to gain and maintain power. In this respect, Machiavelli's *Prince* resembles Hobbes' *Leviathan*: both deal with the problem of creating order out of chaos, and both find the solution in an absolutist state. In his longer book, *Discourses on Livy*, it becomes clear that Machiavelli considers the absolutist principality to be a most primitive form of government. He treats it as a first stage in an historical evolution. A prince needs to be ruthless to create order. But if he is wise, he will instill in his citizens civic virtues which will allow them to engage responsibly in the making of laws and the administration of certain functions. Forms of government change. If conditions are right, a principality may evolve into less autocratic forms of government and finally emerge as a Republic.[19]

Machiavelli's *Discourses* presented a vision in which a principality might mature into a Republic: an ideal form of rule based on education, civic virtue, and popular participation. Later writers retained Machiavelli's republican ideal while refining his theory of historical evolution. Francis Bacon (1561–1626), one of Machiavelli's British admirers, introduced a more explicit theory of progress, emphasizing the importance of Reason as driving forces of History. In *The Advancement of Learning*, Bacon claimed that human knowledge was steadily expanding and that quality of human life was improving.[20]

When Bacon published his book (in 1605), this was a controversial claim. The more common argument at the time was that the ancient civilizations of Greece and Rome were superior to those of modern times. By the middle of the century this began to change. By 1700, the debate between the ancients and the moderns had no obvious winner.[21] But as the new century evolved, a consensus emerged that human knowledge was steadily improving. As the idea of Progress came to dominate, so-called stage-theories emerged. Jean-Jacques Rousseau, for example, described human history in terms of an evolution from a primitive state of nature through agrarian to commercial stages of development.

When David Hume, an ardent admirer of Rousseau, returned from several productive years in France, he brought with him several essays. One of them was a devastating critique of the social-contract theories of Hobbes and Locke. Hume brushed aside as pure fiction the idea that orderly societies were products of reason-based contracts. He argued instead that families, clans, and other small human groups had always existed and that they had grown more numerous because of needs for protection and defense. They had been refined by social divisions of labor—from primitive tribes, through chieftainships and kingdoms to monarchies.[22] Hume's good friend, Adam Smith, relied on the same basic idea to formulate a stage-theory of economic development—primitive societies of hunters–gatherers had evolved into societies of shepherds, which in time gave way to societies based on agriculture and, finally, to economies of industry and commerce. Each new stage would be more productive and wealthier than the last.

Notions of change and historical Progress were implicit in eighteenth-century arguments which championed revolutionary change. They may be glimpsed in *Common Sense*, Thomas Paine's incendiary advocacy for revolution from 1776, and in the preamble of the American Declaration of Independence. It notes how "in the course of human events, it becomes necessary for one people to dissolve the political bands which have connected them with another...." A similar mindset is evident in German philosopher Immanuel Kant's 1784 effort to answer the question "What Is Enlightenment?". His short answer was that "Enlightenment is man's emergence from his self-incurred immaturity." His longer answer defined Enlightenment as a combination of courage, knowledge, and revolutionary Progress: If humankind dares to pursue knowledge, Kant averred, then it can break the shackles of despotism everywhere.

For Kant, the Enlightenment was a vast, reason-based, self-liberating project. As a motto for the Enlightenment, he proposed *Sapere aude!* ("Dare to know," or "Have the courage to use your own Reason"). A comparable idea is implicit in Paine's *Common Sense* from 1776. The idea of Progress is more fully developed in his more impressive work *Rights of Man*, written 15 years later. Paine's list of the basic Rights refers to "liberty, property, security, and resistance of oppression"—very similar to those mentioned by Locke. The American Revolution intended to institute these inalienable Rights. And the sole purpose of government is to safeguard them. Then he adds that these ideals, which drove the American Revolution of 1776, have since spread to Europe. Paine notes how they have just toppled royal despotism in France and argues that they will continue to spread from one country to the other and topple tyrants everywhere.

1.3   Ideal–Typical Representatives

The Enlightenment emerged from the Age of Reason. Its characteristics and attributes were suggested during the Italian Renaissance and grew more visible later in societies along the North Atlantic rim. This happened first in the Netherlands during the later phases of the Thirty Years' Wars, where it was shaped by Simon Stevin, Hugo Grotius, Benedictus de Spinoza, René Descartes, Thomas Hobbes, and others. Soon thereafter it struck roots in England, Scotland, and North America.

Who would be an ideal–typical representative of the Enlightenment? Isaac Newton is an obvious candidate. He was one of the most celebrated scientists of the age. He developed, among other things, the concept of gravity, which allowed him to construct a mathematical model of the solar system, complete with the elliptic orbits of its planets. Through his observations, his model of the universe, his long directorship of London's Royal Society, and through the force of his example, Newton made formidable contributions to the Enlightenment. However, his contribution was to natural Philosophy. Newton was not a moral philosopher. His system paid no attention to the central Enlightenment idea of Rights, let alone the moral law. Better representatives for the moral Philosophy of the age, then, would be Algernon Sidley and John Locke, discussed in the next chapter.

Sidney was a politician and a diplomat who, after travels in Rome, Paris, and Brussels, developed an admiration for Machiavelli's republicanism, Grotian law and popular government, and a dislike for the absolutism of Robert Filmer and Thomas Hobbes. Locke expressed similar preferences, but he wrote a few years later than Sidney. Locke was influenced by more modern Dutch and English thinkers.[23] He was, for example, influenced by Descartes, Robert Boyle, and scientific publications from the London Royal Society—especially those of Isaac Newton (whose writings Sidney never read). Indeed, Locke was so inspired by Newton that he sought to apply the scientific method of Newton's Natural Philosophy to the field of Moral Philosophy. Where Newton placed the abstract concept of "gravity" at the center of his theory of the universe, Locke developed the concept of "Natural Rights" and made it the core principle of his theory of government.[24]

Locke's moral philosophy was further developed by Francis Hutcheson and Adam Smith. Both were professors of Moral Philosophy at Glasgow University and good representatives of the Scottish Enlightenment. Thomas Paine may be an even better ideal–typical exponent of the Enlightenment spirit, together with William and Mary Godwin. All three were optimistic about the powers of human Reason and the way it could shape the human future. Also, they were deeply concerned with questions of equality, justice, and Rights. They argued that society could be greatly improved if the government of the country were to realize and protect the Rights of its citizens.

William Goodwin, produced a steady stream of poetry, novels, journalism, history, demography, and political philosophy which, inspired by Rousseau, was critical and oppositional. Godwin's *Enquiry Concerning Political Justice* (1793) was written under the inspiration of the French Revolution and portrays government as an oppressive and indoctrinating force. It argues that government prevents progress through social practices which uphold property, marriage, and monarchy.

This was very much in tune with Mary Wollstonecraft, whom he married in 1797. She, too, wrote prolifically. Among her works were novels, travelogues, children's books, a history of the French Revolution, and political treatises. In her most famous treatise, *A Vindication of the Rights of Woman* (1792), she argued that women are not naturally inferior to men but appear to be so only because they have been deprived of education. William and Mary Godwin envisioned a future society founded on equal Rights, in which men and women should both receive an education that would develop them as rational human beings. By the free use of their Reason, members of this society would establish an order with freedom and justice for all.

The Godwins knew of Thomas Paine. He had eked out a humble existence in England as a frustrated clerk and a petty bureaucrat until he met Benjamin Franklin—another good candidate for the ideal–typical Enlightenment man. Paine emigrated to Philadelphia on Franklin's invitation. He arrived in 1774, when discussions of American self-government ran high on the heels of the Boston Tea Party. Paine brought with him the ideas of Sidney and a radical interpretation of Locke's *Two Treatises of Government*. He wrote well and quickly made a name as a publicist and editor of *The Pennsylvania Magazine*. Upon the publication of his pamphlet *Common Sense* (1776), Paine emerged as an enthusiastic proponent of American sovereignty and a key propagandist of an American Revolution. Benjamin Franklin, Thomas Jefferson, and James Madison are also good representatives of the Moral Philosophy of the Enlightenment. They have tended to overshadow Paine. He was, however, a more substantial thinker than his *Common Sense* might suggest. His visionary radicalism is apparent in *The Rights of Man* (1791/1792), a two-volume work which he wrote to defend the French Revolution against critics and detractors. Paine explicitly took his former friend, Edmund Burke, to task, arguing that the ideals of the American Revolution had spread to France, and that they would continue to spread progressively—from America and France to other regions of the globe. In Paine's mind, Reason- and Rights-based arguments would sweep away autocratic rulers everywhere and progressively liberate popular masses all over the world.

Thomas Jefferson and Madison held similar but more tempered views.[25] Jefferson was influenced by Hutcheson and the Scotsman's theory of a Reason-derived moral sense of justice and right. It provided a foundation for Jefferson's distaste for aristocracy and his trust in the common farmer. When Jefferson described the difference between himself and his Federalist opponents (such as Alexander Hamilton), he wrote that whereas he (Jefferson) feared the selfishness of rulers, his opponents feared the ignorance of the people[26]; whereas he believed in progress—in "the improvability of the human mind, in science, in ethics and government, &c"—they denied that such improvement was possible and placed their trust in custom and tradition.[27]

Texts by Paine and Jefferson reverberate with ideas of a "moral sense" based on Reason and Rights and driving human Progress. These ideas caused Paine to reject religion and Jefferson to think that Jesus needed to be rescued from organized Christianity.[28] They sustained deist beliefs which Paine and Jefferson shared with Benjamin Franklin, George Washington, John Adams, James Madison, and others.[29] It is worth noting that the majority of the American population probably held religious views which were in tune with the more fundamentalist faith of the Pilgrim Fathers—as indicated by the evangelic awakening that swept America during the first quarter of the nineteenth century. Yet, they embraced the ideas of Progress, Reason, and Right.

The opening paragraph of the Declaration of Independence presents human history as a progressive course of events, governed by "the laws of nature and of nature's God." The second specifies that these natural laws include equality, reason, and rights. It is one of the most famous formulations of American political philosophy. It also distils in a single drop of crystal-clear language, the essence of the Enlightenment:

> We hold these truths to be self-evident: That all men are created equal; that they are endowed by their creator with certain unalienable Rights; that among these are life, liberty, and the pursuit of happiness; that to secure these rights, governments are instituted among men, deriving their just powers from the consent of the governed, ..."[30]

1.4   Concluding Caveat

The Enlightenment was not one thing. It was many. It was rich and varied, so it may be misleading to select a few individuals as ideal–typical representatives. The Enlightenment expressed itself differently in different countries. The Dutch and the Scottish Enlightenments were practical and pragmatic. The English Enlightenment was colorful and varied. The French polished and radical—the French sharpened the Dutch and English arguments into extreme and ostentatious arguments.[31]

The Enlightenment evolved in societies along the North Atlantic rim. And the argument can be made, that although its evolution took place along its European shore, the Enlightenment achieved its most characteristic and lasting form in North America.

Notes

1. Niccolò Machiavelli, *The Prince* (Harmondsworth: Penguin, [1629] 1961), chapter 25.
2. The most famous effort was made by Hugo Grotius, who wrote his monumental *Rights of War and Peace* while the Thirty Years' War raged around him. He hoped that human beings might use their reason to agree to legal limits to the destruction of war. The book is commonly seen as having started the development of modern International Law—Hugo Grotius, *The Rights of War and Peace* (London: M. Walter Dunne (1901 [1625])).
3. Adam Smith, Immanuel Kant, and several other thinkers cut their academic teeth on Newton's theories and published works on planetary orbits before they branched into moral Philosophy.

4. Some of the earliest British novelists were women who wrote exotic tales inspired by early colonialism—as reflected, e.g., in the title of Margaret Cavendish' novel *The Description of the New World* (1666) and Aphra Behn's *Oroonoko: Or the Royal Slave* (1688). Defoe's immensely successful *Robinson Crusoe* (1719) may be read as a novel of colonial trade and exploration but also as a celebration of human ingenuity. Swift's *Gulliver's Travels* (1726) may be read as a satire.

5. Publicists were often sharply critical—as in the cases of Voltaire, Rousseau, and Diderot; and as demonstrated by Mary Wollstonecraft and her husband William Godwin. See Mary Wollstonecraft, *A Vindication of the Rights of Women* (London: Dover [1792] 1996); and William Godwin, Enquiry *Concerning Political Justice and Its Influence on Morals and Happiness* (London: Penguin [1793] 1996).

6. There were waves of witch-hunting in both Europe and America well into the eighteenth century. The last execution for witchcraft in England took place in 1716—before the Witchcraft Act of 1735 put an end to the practice. In Catholic countries, the Institution continued for another century. In France it was abolished in the wake of the Napoleonic Wars.

7. Hugo Grotius, *The Free Sea* (Minneapolis: Liberty Fund, [1609] 2004).

8. Francis Hutcheson, *An Inquiry into the Original of Our Ideas of Beauty and Virtue* (Minneapolis: Liberty Fund, [1726] 2004).

9. Francis Hutcheson, *A Short Introduction to Moral Philosophy* (Minneapolis-St. Paul: Liberty Fund, [1747] 2007).

10. For Descartes the way to true knowledge went through meditation and systematic doubt. In his search for a foundation of true knowledge, Descartes threw into doubt *all* knowledge—except that of the mind itself in the process of thinking. Because, for Descartes, to doubt is to think, and to think means to exist. In his mind, he could not doubt that he existed, since he was doing the doubting in the first place. He summarized his insight in his famous dictum, "I think, therefore I am"—*cogito ergo sum*.

11. Thomas Hobbes, *Leviathan* (Harmondsworth: Penguin, [1651], 1951), chapters VII and IX.

12. See an elaboration in Francis Fukuyama, *Identity* (London: Profile Books, 2019), chapter 3 (pp. 25ff.).

13. If a state is based on religion, clerics will be either masters or servants of rulers. In any case, they will inevitably quarrel, and rival sects will fight to gain control of the state, argued Locke.
14. Property is already implicit in Hobbes' formulation of natural Rights (see, e.g., *Leviathan*, Chapter XV, "Natural Right versus Natural Law"). Hobbes argues that to be a free and freely thinking human being, a person must possess enough property as to ensure independence from others. The importance of private property is also indicated in Hobbes' claim that in the state of nature there is no difference between "mine and thine," but that when the state of nature has been superseded by a social contract, such a distinction is made by an all-powerful Leviathan as a measure of keeping social order.
15. Locke's labor theory of property (or more correctly, his "labor theory of appropriation"), holds that property is created when an individual works with natural resources and "mixes his labour with" those resources. This theory has had a profound influence on Classical Political Economy in England (e.g., on Adam Smith, David Ricardo, and Karl Marx). It was also used to justify England's colonialism—most explicitly the expansion of English settlements in north America.
16. See John Locke, "A Letter Concerning Toleration", in *A Letter Concerning Toleration and Other Writings* (Indianapolis: Liberty Fund, [1685] 2010), pp. 1–69. The argument is more explicitly developed by others—especially by Rousseau and other Continental thinkers.
17. This optimistic argument is part of a liberal tradition. A second, more pessimistic argument is part of a radical political tradition: That if the extant world is so full of injustices and oppression, it must mean that they are affected by unjust and oppressive experiences from the cultural and institutional environment into which each individual was born.
18. However, some thinkers added that Reason is affected by the social conditions that surrounds the individual. This was the argument of Rousseau, who claimed that society could shape and corrupt the natural workings of Reason. For this corruption he blamed the wider cultural environment of the West. Other French philosophers argue along similar lines. César Dumarsais is one. A more famous

example is Voltaire, who lies the responsibility for this alienation at the door of the Catholic Church and the French monarchy.

19. If conditions are not right, Republics may deteriorate to oligarchies or even principalities. Machiavelli, *Discourses on Livy* (Oxford: Oxford University Press, [1517] 1997), esp. chapter 2.

20. Francis Bacon, *The Advancement of Learning* (London: Cassell & Company, [1605] 1893).

21. In 1750 economist and statesman Anne Robert Turgot outlined a complete doctrine of progress. Forty years later, his young friend and disciple, Marquis de Condorcet, wrote an optimistic sketch of the steady progress of humankind from the primitive conditions of the past toward a utopia of universal wellbeing and peace in the future. See Marquis de Condorcet, *Esquisse d'un tableau historique des progrès de l'esprit humain* (Paris: Flammarion, [1795] 1988).

22. David Hume, "Of the Origin of Government", in *Essays, Moral, Political and Literary* (Indianapolis: Liberty Classics [1741] 1985), pp. David Hume, *A Treatise of Human Nature* (Oxford: Clarendon Press [1740] 1978), Book 3, Part 2. Sections VII and VIII.

23. Locke spent five years of voluntary exile in Holland, where he became familiar with a circle of freethinking followers of Spinoza. This sharpened his opposition against absolutist monarchy—he was skeptical of Hobbes absolutism and explicitly hostile toward Robert Filmer. While in Holland, Locke was also affected by René Descartes. When he returned to England, he admired the publications of the London Royal Society. He was inspired by Isaac Newton's philosophy of science.

24. Graham A. J. Rogers, "Locke's Essay and Newton's Principia", in *Journal of the History of Ideas*, Vol. 39, No. 2 (1978), pp. 217–232.

25. On the political philosophies of the Founding Fathers, see e.g., Joseph Ellis, *Founding Brothers: The Revolutionary Generation* (New York: Knopf, 2001); and Adrienne Koch, *Jefferson, and Madison: The Great Collaboration* (New York: Knopf, 1950).

26. Thomas Jefferson, "Letter to Abigal Adams", 11 September 1804. In *Political Writings* (Cambridge: Cambridge University Press, 1999), p. 42.

27. Jefferson, "Letter to Adams", 15 June 1813, in *ibid.*, p. 574; p. xiii.

28. Jefferson,"Letter to William Short", 4 August 1820, in *ibid.*, pp. 401ff.
29. See David L. Holmes, *The Faiths of the Founding Fathers* (Oxford: Oxford University Press, 2006). Holmes makes the point that there are varieties of deism. But a common denominator is, the view that nature itself sufficiently demonstrate the existence of God, making formal, established religion unnecessary. Simply put, they held that a Creator made an orderly universe governed by natural laws and thereafter left it to run on its own like a well-manufactured clock. See e.g., Donald W. Viney, "American Deism, Christianity, and the Age of Reason", in *American Journal of Theology & Philosophy*, Vol. 31, No. 2 (2010), pp. 83–107.
30. Jefferson, "The Declaration of Independence", *Political Writings*, pp. 102–105.
31. The German Enlightenment evolved relatively late, and developed characteristics which were uniquely its own. See Sabrina P. Ramet and Torbjørn L. Knutsen, *German Moral and Political Philosophy, 1785–1908: A Concise Introduction*, with an afterword by Jonathon W. Moses (Washington, D.C.: New Academia Publishing, 2023).

FURTHER READINGS

Bell, Duncan. "What Is Liberalism?", in *Political Theory*, Vol. 42, No. 6 (December 2014).

Gottlieb, Anthony. *The Dream of Enlightenment: The Rise of Modern Philosophy* (Penguin, 2017).

Israel, Jonathan. "Enlightenment! Which Enlightenment?", in *Journal of the History of Ideas*, Vol. 67, No. 3 (July 2006).

Kenny, Anthony. *The Enlightenment: A Very Brief History* (SPCK, 2017).

Kors, Alan Charles (ed.-in-chief). *Encyclopedia of the Enlightenment*, 4 vols. (Oxford University Press, 2003).

Pagden, Anthony. *The Enlightenment: And Why It Still Matters* (Oxford University Press, 2015).

Robertson, John. *The Enlightenment: A Very Short Introduction* (Oxford University Press, 2015).

CHAPTER 2

The English Enlightenment: Algernon Sidney and John Locke

Sabrina P. Ramet

Abstract Algernon Sidney and John Locke were (together with Benedictus de Spinoza and Samuel von Pufendorf) among the earliest advocates of the central tenets of the Enlightenment, i.e., reliance on Reason, respect for the Moral Law, and active engagement to expand people's Freedom and Rights. Sidney and Locke shared a common antagonist in Sir Robert Filmer, whose posthumously published tract, *Patriarcha*, defended absolutism by reference to Scripture. Both men demanded a greater role for parliament and, for Locke in particular, liberal politics entailed (a limited form of) religious toleration. Both men wrote that kings and governments should be accountable to the people, rather than the reverse, and justified popular resistance to a king who abused his power. They appealed to Universal Reason (or Natural Law) to support their arguments for political freedom and greater rights for people.

Keywords Popular resistance · Universal Reason · Natural duties · Rule of law · Revolution · Rye House Plot · Secular government

Algernon Sidney (1622–1683) and John Locke (1632–1704) fought for revolution both through direct action and through their writings. They

S. P. Ramet and T. L. Knutsen, *Key Thinkers of the English, Scottish and American Enlightenments*,
https://doi.org/10.1007/978-3-031-62454-4_2

appealed to *Reason* (with Locke devoting his magisterial *Essay on Human Understanding* to this theme), to lay the foundation for their advocacy of basic *Rights*, including the right to resist an oppressive monarch. Both Sidney and Locke, but especially the latter, appealed to the *Moral Law* to support their case against what they considered tyranny. Although they were opposing the claims of the monarchy in England, their influence extended not only to England but also to North America, where their ideas provided inspiration for the American Revolution and contributed ideas to the American Founding Fathers, who read the works of both Sidney and Locke with care and interest. In the early years of the American Republic, Algernon Sidney was hailed as the greater hero, but, with time, his star has dimmed. Today Locke figures as a dominant influence and remains one of the three most influential liberals from the eighteenth and nineteenth centuries, alongside Immanuel Kant and John Stuart Mill.

2.1   THE ENLIGHTENMENT

The Enlightenment gave birth to and nurtured a deep, abiding confidence in the power of Reason, and, accompanying it, an acceptance of the moral principles of Natural Law (which Locke called Universal Reason) and natural rights, which, in turn, entailed natural duties. The chief principles of the Enlightenment included the demands for religious toleration, government responsible to the people, freedom of thought and of the press, freedom of assembly, separation of powers, the rule of law, secular government, and free public education. The Enlightenment was a period of roughly 150 years, stretching from the mid-seventeenth century to the end of the eighteenth century, in which reason, science, and humanism (the championing of the value of human life) were ascendant. It was a European and North American phenomenon, with its main centers in England, Scotland, France, the German states, and the United States, but with advocates and influence throughout the European continent, including in Holland, Prussia, the Habsburg Empire (Austria), Italy, Portugal, Spain, Serbia, Sweden, Poland, and Russia. The English Enlightenment may be considered to have begun with Sidney, Locke, and James Tyrrell (1642–1718), although it had been foreshadowed in the 1640s, with the appearance in England of the Independents (or Levellers) who championed the supremacy of law and freedom of Christian religion. The demand registered by Sidney and Locke for the rule of law and by Locke for religious toleration pitted them against the prerogatives claimed by the King. The appeal to reason eroded the traditional hierarchy of classes, as demands for equality came to be voiced, and undercut the Christian Churches' appeal to divine authority.

2.2 ALGERNON SIDNEY

In the decades following his execution in 1683, Algernon Sidney enjoyed huge posthumous influence in England, France, and America, and was read by Montesquieu, Benjamin Franklin, and American Presidents John Adams and Thomas Jefferson, among others. His most influential work, *Discourses concerning Government*, published posthumously in 1698, offered a bolder defense of a people's right to rebel than John Locke did. Not wanting to defend rebellion against the monarch explicitly, Locke cautiously cast the monarch's alleged abuse of power as constituting a rebellion on the part of the monarch against the people, thereby justifying resistance to the King's supposed rebellion against the laws of the land (for discussion, see below). By contrast, Sidney defended the right of rebellion by the people and explicitly justified the removal of kings when they failed in their duties.[1] For at least half a century after his death, when it came to defenses of popular government, Sidney was cited in England at least as often as Locke, while in America enthusiasm for him reached such a pitch in some circles that a nineteenth-century politician in Massachusetts would declare Sidney "an American name – American in all its associations and American in all its influences."[2] In 1825, at Thomas Jefferson's urging, as founder of the University of Virginia, the board of visitors of the university passed a resolution, declaring that "...it is the opinion of this Board that as to the general principles of liberty and the rights of man, in nature and in society, the doctrines of Locke, in his *Essay concerning the true original extent and end of civil government*, and of Sidney in his *Discourses on government*, may be considered as those generally approved by your fellow citizens of this [state], and the United States."[3] By the end of the nineteenth century, however, Algernon Sidney had fallen into oblivion.

His Life and Political Engagement

Sidney was born in 1622, second son of Robert, Earl of Leicester, and Dorothy Percy, daughter of the Earl of Northumberland. His great-uncle was Sir Philip Sidney (1554–1586), a soldier, poet, and author of *The*

Countess of Pembroke's Arcadia, whose own radicalism would later be forgotten. At the time that the English Civil War broke out, Algernon Sidney was only 20 years of age and, at that point in time, was undecided between King and Parliament. Subsequently, he enlisted in Oliver Cromwell's army (see Box 2.1) and participated in the Battle of Marston Moor in 1644, in which the Royalist army was dealt a severe blow.

Box 2.1: Oliver Cromwell

Oliver Cromwell (1599–1658), who presided from 1653 until his death in 1658 over England, Scotland, and Ireland as Lord Protector, was born in Huntingdon, Cambridgeshire, studied at the University of Cambridge, and represented Huntingdon in parliament from 1628 to 1629. In the 1630s, he converted to radical Puritanism, and in 1640 returned to parliament, representing Cambridge. When civil war broke out between King Charles I and the parliament in 1642, Cromwell joined the parliamentary army and led an effective cavalry force, rising from captain to lieutenant-general in just three years. Eventually, Cromwell became commander of the parliamentary army and Lord Lieutenant of Ireland; facing resistance in Ireland, he massacred those resisting at Drogheda and Wexford in 1649. With his victory over the remaining royalist forces, now supporting Charles II, son of the executed Charles I, at Dunbar (1650) and Worcester (1651), the civil war came to an end. Two years later, Cromwell made himself Lord Protector but, in 1657, declined to accept a crown. As Lord Protector, he reorganized the national Church (abolishing bishops), readmitted Jews into England, introduced some measure of religious tolerance, closed many inns and theaters, and banned most sports.

Sidney stood for election to the House of Commons in 1646 and won a seat representing Cardiff. Then, in 1652, he was elected to the Council of State, where he played a role in fashioning the country's foreign policy. He was out of the country when the republic collapsed and, when Charles II ascended the throne, Sidney, like others, hoped that the new king would accept a limited mandate and be tolerant of dissent, whether religious or political. But the King steered a very different course. In 1662, Sir Henry Vane, a leading parliamentarian whom Sidney admired, was beheaded on charges of high treason, for his prominent role on the side of the Puritans during the Civil War as well as in the Republic. In 1663, Sidney turned up in Switzerland and Holland, where he hoped to recruit political exiles to join a conspiracy against King Charles. Nothing came of this, and he returned to England in 1677. By 1678 there was renewed anti-Catholic hysteria in England, which focused on James, Duke of York, a Catholic and the heir apparent. In the middle of this hysteria, rumors circulated about a "Popish plot" in which Jesuits were allegedly plotting to assassinate King Charles II, murder a large number of Protestants, and put James, the King's brother, on the throne. At this point, Anthony Ashley Cooper, the first Earl of Shaftesbury, introduced a bill to exclude James, the Catholic brother of Charles II and heir presumptive, from the succession. Sidney stood for parliament in the second general election of 1679 and gained a seat in the House of Commons in August of that year, representing Amersham. When the new parliament proved to be as strong-willed as the previous one, the King, having prorogued parliament once before, prorogued this parliament too, on 15 October 1679. Doubts arose concerning the King's intentions and by the end of that year, a petition was being circulated to demand that the King allow parliament to reassemble on 26 January. Sidney and Locke were among the signatories to this petition which was presented to the King in January 1680.[4] The King, however, rejected this petition in advance, and parliament would not meet, in fact, until October 1680. It was in these circumstances that Sidney began writing *Discourses Concerning Government*, arguing that people had both a right and even a duty to depose or kill a tyrant, characterizing the reigning King as one who "despises the law."[5] In 1681, the issue of exclusion was once more raised in the House of Commons, and Charles II once more dissolved the parliament. At this point, rumors about plots and conspiracies circulated widely. One plot which was quite real was the Rye House Plot, which called for assembling a force of 100 men at Rye House, a manor in Hoddesdon, to ambush the King on his way back from horse races. When a fire in Newmarket caused the races to be canceled, the King returned to London early, avoiding the ambush. However, word leaked out and arrests were made. Among those arrested was Algernon Sidney.[6]

Under English law, when the prosecution case rested on testimony alone—as was the case with Algernon Sidney—the prosecution was required to produce at least two witnesses; but the prosecutors could produce only one witness, Lord Howard of Escrick, "whom everyone despised and few trusted."[7] Instead of producing a second witness, however, the prosecution introduced some pages from the unpublished manuscript of *Discourses Concerning Government*, which had been confiscated from Sidney's study when he had been taken into custody. At his trial, Sidney objected that no one should be put on trial for ideas expressed in an unpublished manuscript. However, Sir George Jeffreys, who was presiding as Lord Chief Justice at Sidney's trial, was unsympathetic to the accused, allowed that the stolen pages might serve as a substitute for a second witness, and denied Sidney either legal counsel or a copy of the indictment under which he was being tried.[8] The trial took place on 21 November, and ended with Jeffreys declaring that the defendant had been found guilty of "compassing and imag[in]ing the death of the King."[9] Sentence was passed five days later and carried out on 7 December 1683. As he ascended the scaffold, Sidney passed a prepared text to the sheriff. In this short text, he asserted, inter alia, that it was his belief

> that God had left Nations to the liberty of setting up such Governments as best pleased themselves, and that Magistrates were set up for the good of Nations, not Nations for the honor and glory of Magistrates. That the Right and Power of Magistrates in every Countrey, was that which the Laws of that Countrey made it to be. That these Laws are to be observed, and the Oaths taken by Rulers to be kept. And that having the Force of contracts between Magistrates and People, they can not be violated without danger of dissolving the whole Fabrick. That Usurpations can give no Right...This is the Scope of the whole Treatise [Discourses], and...[t]his seems to agree with the Doctrines of the most renown'd Authors of all times, Nations and Religions.[10]

Sidney was beheaded with a single blow.

Sidney's Discourses Concerning Government

Algernon Sidney's *Discourses* should be seen both as a response to the King's prorogation of four parliaments and as a response to the posthumous publication of Sir Robert Filmer's *Patriarcha* in 1680. Filmer championed the supposed divine right of kings, a theory which had been developed to place the authority of kings beyond challenge by the citizens he ruled. Thus, for example, in a crucial passage in *Patriarcha*, Filmer argued that

> Men are not born free, and therefore could never have the liberty to choose either [their] Governors, or Forms of Government. Princes have their Power Absolute, and by Divine Right, for Slaves could never have a

Right to Compact or Consent. Adam was an absolute Monarch, and so are all Princes ever since.[11]

Filmer's book was, quite transparently, useful to Charles II and his supporters, with its defense of royal prerogative, its broadsides against claims of natural liberty, and its attacks on classical republics. But even before turning to the work on *Discourses,* Sidney brought out a shorter work, entitled *A Just and Modest Vindication of the Proceedings of the Two Last Parliaments* (published in 1681). In *Vindication,* Sidney pleaded that kings had been granted their authority only to serve the good of the people.[12]

Sidney probably began writing *Discourses* in the second half of 1681, and, by the time of his arrest in May 1683, he had written 508 pages of text. His emphasis throughout the *Discourses* was on people's right to self-government through elected representatives and their right to resist absolutism by any means necessary and useful to that end. The doctrine of the divine right of kings had received an early challenge from Niccolò Machiavelli (1469–1527) who in the *Discourses,* he contrasted Christian religion unfavorably with the old polytheist Olympian religion,[13] and held that well-run states deal justly with all their citizens, regardless of their social class. Here his sympathies clearly lay with the common people since, in his view, they wanted "only to avoid being oppressed," while the noble class wanted to dominate and oppress ordinary people.[14] Furthermore, for Machiavelli, "a minimal constitutional order is one in which subjects live securely (*vivere sicuro*), ruled by a strong government which holds in check the aspirations of both nobility and people, but is, in turn, balanced by other legal and institutional mechanisms." "In a fully constitutional regime, however, the goal of the political order is the freedom of the community (*vivere libero*), created by the active participation of, and contention between, the nobility and the people."[15] Although he drew his inspiration from the Roman Republic, Machiavelli sometimes sounded modern in his defense of republicanism. At that time, the influence of Hugo Grotius (1583–1645) was perhaps at its peak. Sometimes regarded as one of the most important philosophers in the early modern era to advocate and explicate Natural Law, Grotius understood that Law as both descriptive (what people do or tend to do) and prescriptive (i.e., as the moral law).[16] In seeking to uphold the divine right of kings, Filmer had to refute both Machiavelli's republicanism and Grotius' elevation of Natural Law above kings and queens. It was with these thinkers in mind that Filmer argued that people were born unfree (in subjection to their parents and their kings) and derided both Grotius' Natural Law theory and Machiavelli's republicanism. Sidney, tellingly, applauded both Grotius's theory of Natural Law and the republicanism of Machiavelli, harnessing the former in defense of the latter. In advancing his argument, Sidney organized it as a reply to Filmer's *Patriarcha*, responding point by point.

For Filmer, as a result of the Fall (meaning the original sin of Adam in the Garden of Eden, taken literally), all people are born into sin, so that the purpose of government should be seen as the restraint of sin. By multiplying the number of participants in political life, the popular rule would risk multiplying wickedness.[17] Sidney, on the other hand, emphasized the human capacity for moral reasoning and held that governments were set up for the purpose of promoting the good of all members of society.[18] Thus, where Filmer equated liberty with an opening for sinfulness, Sidney countered that liberty did not mean that people could do whatever they pleased, but signified only "an exemption for all human laws, to which they have not given their assent."[19] Again, where Filmer had claimed that people should obey their King in all things and not question anything, Sidney responded that, on the contrary, "the King should be subject to the censures of the people."[20] For Filmer, royal authority derived from the patriarchal authority of fathers and from specific appointment by God to rule. For Sidney, kings enjoy their authority at the pleasure of their subjects. As he put it in Chapter 1 of *Discourses*:

> if governments arise from the consent of men, and are instituted by men according to their own inclinations, they do therein seek their own good; for the will is ever drawn by some real good, or the appearance of it...A people therefore that sets up kings, dictators, consuls, pretors or emperors, does it not, that they may be great, glorious, rich or happy, but that it may be well with themselves and their posterity.[21]

More to the point, it was not for the magistrate (the King) to judge whether or not he was executing the duties of his office properly. On the contrary, it could only be the people themselves who could judge whether the magistrate had worked for the public good or not.[22]

Filmer had thought that hereditary succession was the best assurance of good government, but Sidney countered that such a mechanism was no assurance of good rule, and that, on the contrary, a country operating under such a system was virtually guaranteed to fall under the governance of a rogue or an idiot from time to time. And where Filmer had claimed that mixed monarchy was a contradiction in terms, and that the choice was between monarchy (in an absolutist form) and rule by the people (democracy), Sidney disagreed and held out for a variety of forms of government, including limited monarchy.[23] What limited monarchy meant to Sidney was, in the first place, that the monarch was subject to the law of the land, not above the law, and likewise subject to the moral law, which Sidney defended against Filmer's attempt to dismiss it as an illusion. Sidney had argued this point likewise in *Court Maxims,* demanding that public law be in harmony with both Divine Law and Natural Law; this betrays the fact that Sidney was a deeply religious man.[24] "[T]he power [princes] have, ought to be limited by law," he wrote, adding that he found "it impossible to [believe]…that kings may govern as they please,…or that princes can attempt to dissolve the obligations laid upon them by the laws, which they so solemnly swear to observe, without rendering themselves detestable to God and man."[25] In this connection, Sidney referred to Hobbes, giving him credit for having been the first to have "contrived a compendious way of justifying the most abominable perjuries, and all the mischiefs ensuing thereupon, by pretending, that as the king's oath is made to the people, the people may absolve him from the obligation [imposed by that oath]; and that the people have conferred upon him all the power they had, he can do all that they could: he can therefore absolve himself, and is actually free, since he is so when he pleases."[26] This linkage of Filmer with Hobbes was a piece of polemical genius since it placed the knighted author of *Patriarcha* in the same company with an author who was widely viewed as an atheist and who had been condemned in many circles.

Although Sidney objected to absolute monarchy, he came to admire King Charles X of Sweden, who, he felt, used his power to advance the public interest.[27] But this serves to remind us that, for Sidney, public virtue—including the virtue of the magistrate—was more important than the structure of power. Here he contrasted the virtue of self-control with the corruption (or vice) of licentiousness and unbridled self-indulgence, the virtue of martial valor with the corruption of weakness, and the virtue of integrity with the corruption of violating the public trust. The problem with absolute monarchy was that, if a monarch should prove less than virtuous, it afforded no checks on a monarch's complete self-indulgence in whatever might please him. And although "…Sidney certainly believed that whole classes of people were plainly unfit to exercise political power and plainly incapable of giving their own consent to government,"[28] and denied that there was any universally valid form of government,[29] there were several criteria for good government in his view. These were that government be limited, that it seeks to advance the public good while remaining responsive to the popular will and govern by reason, and that it be committed to fight corruption. The consent of the government was also a requirement of good government, in Sidney's view.

Sidney defended Natural Law as a source of general understanding of the importance of standing by one's oaths. He also defended the popular right to free assembly, the right of parliament to sit in session and not to be dismissed arbitrarily when its deliberations created difficulties for the king, and the right of the people both to choose and to dismiss their king. Finally, tracing the word "rebel" to the Latin "rebellare," meaning to renew a war, Sidney argued that people have a right to rebel when the magistrate works against the common good, and indeed that rebellion is not always evil but may work for the better for the community.[30] Furthermore, where one might suppose that succession within a hereditary dynasty might be an assurance of stability, Sidney argued that, on the contrary, "Popular Governments are less subject to Civil Disorders than Monarchies; manage them more ably, and more easily recover out of them." Indeed, even while conceding that "there is a sort of sedition, tumult, and war proceeding from malice, which is always detestable, aiming only at the satisfaction of private lust, without regard to the public good," he assured his readers that "[t]his cannot happen in a popular government, unless it be amongst the rabble; or when the body of the people is so corrupted, that it cannot stand; but is most frequent in, and natural to, absolute monarchies."[31]

For its time, Sidney's tract was indeed revolutionary and was certainly intended to subvert the foundations of absolutist monarchy. There is little surprise then that, after the Glorious Revolution of 1688 and the ascent of William III of Orange-Nassau and Mary II as King and Queen of England, Scotland, and Ireland the following year, supporters of the new crown were eager to cite Sidney in support of the change of dynasty, even claiming that he had sown the "seed" for the Glorious Revolution. But this interpretation was flawed since, in his *Court Maxims, Refuted and Refelled*, written in the mid-1660s and discovered in Warwick Castle only in 1976, Sidney had called for the extirpation of both the Stuart and the Orange dynasties.[32] Sidney would have found the "Glorious Revolution," which brought the Orange dynasty which he reviled to England, abhorrent.

2.3 JOHN LOCKE

Like Sidney, Locke was knee-deep in politics, prominent in the opposition, and on the King's most wanted list. Indeed, Richard Ashcraft suggests that Locke was almost definitely involved in the Rye House Plot. One piece of evidence cited by Ashcraft is that, within less than a month of the Newmarket fire (March 1683) which allowed the King to escape immediate danger, Locke paid a visit to the Earl of Essex, who was one of the Council of Six who were overseeing the conspiracy (which, however, Houston suggests got out of their control).[33] The earl was arrested and died in the Tower of London under mysterious circumstances, while awaiting his trial. Locke's friend, the Earl of Shaftesbury, had died at the beginning of the year, but it was his plans for insurrection that the Council of Six was trying to implement. Locke, who had drawn up his own defense of resistance to royal oppression in *Two Treatises of Government*, was worried. Several of his close associates in the opposition had been arrested, as well as Shaftesbury's erstwhile servant and a member of Shaftesbury's family. By August, some of the conspirators had been executed, among them both Sidney and Lord Russell, and, after selling the deed to a farm left to him by Shaftesbury for £500, Locke fled the country, arriving in Rotterdam on 7 September 1683.[34] He would not return to England until 1689.

His Life and Political Activity

Locke was born in 1632 at Wrington in Somerset into an undistinguished family of local officials and landowners. As a Presbyterian, he had joined the parliamentary army during the English Civil War. Locke began his education at Westminster School[35]; his educational attainments there propelled him into Oxford University in 1652, at the age of 20. At Oxford, Locke pursued a traditional course of study, including Aristotelian logic, metaphysics, classical languages, medicine, and chemistry. Indeed, in the 15 years Locke spent at Oxford, most of his study time was devoted to medicine and chemistry.

At this time, Locke's thinking about politics and religion was very conservative.[36] In writings from the years 1660–1662, Locke favored the hard line taken by the reestablished Church of England against all forms of dissent, thereby aligning himself with the very establishment against which his father had fought. In the summer of 1666, Locke made the acquaintance of Anthony Ashley Cooper, the later Earl of Shaftesbury. The following year, Lord Ashley (as he was called until 1672) asked Locke to join him in London, to serve as his personal physician.[37] Locke became more than merely a personal physician to Ashley. He became his confidant/counselor, personal secretary, and close political collaborator. Lord Ashley was a strong opponent of arbitrary and absolutist government. Working with Ashley, Locke reworked and refined his views about religious toleration and other matters, and gravitated toward the defense of revolution. Ashley was, in particular, opposed to the Clarendon Code (see Box 2.2), the set of repressive legislation against religious dissenters passed by the Anglican-dominated parliaments during the first half of the 1660s.

Box 2.2: The Clarendon Code
Passed during the ministry of Edward Hyde, the first Earl of Clarendon, the Clarendon Code consisted of four legal statutes, adopted by the Anglican-dominated parliament between 1661 and 1665. This limited public office to Anglicans, required the use of the Book of Common Prayer in religious service of the Church of England, banned unauthorized worship of more than five persons who were not living in the same house, and forbade non-Anglican ministers to teach in schools.

As early as 1667, in an essay on toleration, not published in his lifetime, Locke reversed his earlier views and urged that only Catholicism and atheism were necessarily beyond any claim to religious toleration (that is, *among those views being urged in England at the time*). In 1673, James' conversion to Roman Catholicism became public knowledge (James was, at the time, the Duke of York and heir apparent). By 1679, as already mentioned, Ashley (now the Earl of Shaftesbury) was leading a parliamentary campaign to exclude James from the succession. During the next two years, Locke worked closely with Shaftesbury on texts to be included in the subsequently published *Two Treatises of Government*.

During the six years he spent in Holland (1683–1689),[38] Locke made the acquaintance of several latitudinarian theologians; this would have an effect on his thinking. In 1685, after the failure of Monmouth's insurrection, Locke's name appeared on a list of persons who should be arrested and returned for prosecution. Indeed, under James II, English authorities even made an attempt in 1685 to extradite Locke from Holland, and Locke briefly assumed a new identity as "Dr. van der Linden." In 1689–1690, after his return to England, three fruits of his labor in Holland were published: *An Essay Concerning Human Understanding*, *Two Treatises of Government*, and *A Letter Concerning Toleration*. 1695 saw the publication of Locke's controversial *The Reasonableness of Christianity*, the authorship of which Locke never publicly admitted. In 1700, Locke, now age 68, withdrew from all political activities (resigning from the Board of Trade). He died on 28 October 1704, in the company of his close friend Damaris Masham. His reputation as a major, if extremely controversial, philosopher had already been established, both in England and on the Continent.

Locke's Essay Concerning Human Understanding

It might seem remarkable, at first sight, that someone so deeply involved in political opposition should have devoted some years to writing a 1030-page two-volume set about what we can know and how we know it.[39] The explanation for this apparent paradox is that in fighting for certain principles of morality and religion, Locke wanted to be quite certain about exactly what he thought one could actually know about these principles.[40] Rejecting notions that there were some moral principles which were innate in all people—an idea popular in his day and recently revived in a new form by Marc Hauser[41] among others—Locke argued rather that the reason that one could find general agreement on moral principles was that people had the capacity to discern what was moral and what was not moral (which is to say, natural reason). Indeed, Locke expressed confidence that, although one could find variations in moral understandings from one nation or religious group to another, there were nonetheless some moral universals which could be established.[42] Thus, in Book IV of *Essay Concerning Human Understanding*, Locke confidently remarked that "…moral knowledge is as capable of real certainty as mathematics."[43]

Locke was also concerned to give Natural Law—or, rather, the moral component of Natural Law, rather than its empirical component—a secular foundation in reason. Thus, in chapter 9 of his *Second Treatise of Government* he wrote that "the law of nature...[is] plain and intelligible to all rational creatures."[44] Although he granted that he viewed God as commanding obedience to the moral law, he insisted that the validity of the moral law did not depend on God's command. Thus, in the *Essay,* he wrote:

> I doubt not but [that] from self-evident proposition, by necessary consequences, as incontestable as those in mathematics, the measures of right and wrong might be made out, to any one that will apply himself with the same indifferency and attention to the one as he does to the other of these sciences...I cannot see why they should not also be capable of demonstration, if due methods were thought on to examine or pursue their agreement or disagreement.[45]

And against those who fancied that the validity of the moral law depended upon the immortality of the soul and the threat of everlasting punishment (or promise of everlasting reward), Locke replied that, "All the great ends of morality and religion are well enough secured, without philosophical proofs of the soul's immateriality [or immortality]."[46] Moreover, where Hobbes had justified the moral law above all in terms of its utility (in protecting people's lives and giving them some security), Locke wrote that utility, although "the consequence of obedience" to the moral law, was not its foundation.[47]

Locke's Letters on Religious Toleration

The first record we have of Locke's reflecting on religious toleration takes us back to September 1659 when Henry Stubbe, a former fellow schoolmate of Locke's sent the 27-year-old Locke a copy of his recently published essay arguing that the state should not impose any religion on people. Locke read the book and wrote to Stubbe to express his general agreement, indicating reservations only about extending toleration to Catholics, insofar as they owed allegiance to Rome.[48] About a year later, however, Edward Bagshawe published a short pamphlet, *The Great Question concerning things indifferent in religious worship*, in which the author urged that no government had any right to legislate concerning the details of Christian worship—whether, for example, to bow one's head on hearing the name of Jesus of Nazareth. Locke, however, disagreed and, in his *Two Tracts on Government*, worried that, judging from recent experience, the government's failure to regulate certain things "would prove only a liberty for contention, censure and persecution and turn us loose to the tyranny of a religious rage."[49] He considered, at that time, that "...individuals must be supposed to have surrendered their natural liberty and entrusted the ruler with absolute power..."[50] and that the sovereign enjoyed an authority to restrict liberty, derived from God's own authority, and could and should take whatever steps would conduce to the general good of the people. But he was by no means reversing the view he had expressed to Stubbe the previous year and insisted that "conscience is tenderly to be dealt with, and not to be imposed on."[51] But he thought, at the time, that the sovereign was entitled to impose limits on "externals" of ritual and prayer[52]—a position he would reverse later. He also argued that, where the state is considered the legitimate instrument for enforcing true religion, rival clerics and rival sects will inevitably fight in order to gain control of the state.[53]

Soon after Locke joined Shaftesbury's staff in 1667, Shaftesbury asked him to take up the study of ecclesiastical affairs. Shaftesbury's purpose was to acquire intellectual ammunition for the fight against the persecution of religious dissenters in England, which was driving them to emigrate; specifically, Shaftesbury wanted to see the Clarendon Code repealed. The result of this study was an *Essay on Toleration*, completed that same year, in which he declared his interest in the question "whether imposition or toleration be the readiest way to secure the safety and peace...of this kingdom."[54] Locke was, of course, declaring himself in favor of religious toleration, and specifically argued "that speculative opinions and worship which did not affect politics or detract from the public good should *not* be regulated by the magistrate."[55] Since he felt that Catholicism entailed loyalty to a foreign prince (the pope), he concluded that Catholics ought not to enjoy toleration.[56]

Some 22 years later, at the age of 57 and after the death of his friend the Earl of Shaftesbury, Locke wrote and published a much bolder plea for religious toleration—the first of four letters concerning toleration. In the first letter, Locke outlined a vision of a secular state, thereby breaking completely with the medieval tradition as well as with the theory of Richard Hooker, whom Locke would nonetheless cite with favor in *Two Treatises*. For Locke, the concept of the state excluded any religious concern and he warned, in *Letter concerning Toleration*, that "No peace and security, no, not so much as common friendship, can ever be established or preserved amongst men so long as this opinion prevails, 'that dominion is founded in grace and that religion is to be propagated by force of arms.'"[57] And where the Stuarts and the Puritans alike had wanted to use the state to secure and promote the spiritual interests of people, Locke urged, in *Letter*, that a state community should be understood to be "constituted only for the procuring, preserving, and advancing their own civil interests," which he defined as "life, liberty, health, and indolency of body."[58] The civil magistrate had no business, according to Locke, in claiming any jurisdiction or duty to care for the salvation of souls or in judging between the merits of rival churches. On the other hand, the civil magistrate had every right, even the duty, to suppress opinions which were "contrary to human society, or to those moral rules which are necessary to the preservation of civil society."[59] And hence, government was authorized to punish those who would use religious meetings to disturb the public peace, but had no business interfering in the activities of religious bodies where their behavior was "peaceable" and their "manners…pure and blameless."[60]

But Locke needed some additional arguments, besides this, if he was going to make the case that violence on behalf of "the true Church" was unacceptable and that the state should stay out of the business of prescribing religious faith. He offered four arguments: first, that every Church claims to be "true" and that there is no objective way to assess the rival claims; second, that religion is an individual responsibility and the people are not authorized to consent to entrusting the government with authority in this sphere; third, that laws cannot operate without penalties, and penalties are inappropriate in the religious sphere, because penalties do not serve either to persuade or to convince anyone of the truth of religious doctrine; and fourth, that salvation cannot be assured through coercion, since coerced participation in religious rituals cannot be pleasing to any God worth bothering about. On the other hand, Locke justified the use of coercion against Catholics and, "inconsistently with the presuppositions of his own general argument, … maintained that the application of force even carried with it the prospects that Catholics would abandon their religious beliefs and join the ranks of Protestantism."[61]

Locke wanted the government to deny toleration to any sects advocating things which undermined the foundations of society, to any sects advocating that its members lie to non-members or which claimed special political or civic privileges for their members, to any sects whose members owed their primary political loyalty to a foreign prince (this being aimed, as before, at Catholics), and to anyone who denied the existence of God, because atheists allegedly could not be trusted to honor promises, oaths, or agreements. Yet, in spite of his concern about Muslims' loyalty to the sultan, Locke included Muslims on a list of groups to be tolerated, alongside Jews, "pagans," Presbyterians, Anabaptists, Arminians, Quakers, Independents, "and others."

Why is this *Letter concerning Toleration* important? There are at least three reasons: first, because it had considerable readership and influence, and advanced the cause of the secular state; second, because not only liberty, but also equality, depends upon toleration; and third, because the case Locke made for *religious* toleration set a precedent for the defense of other kinds of toleration (e.g., sexual) and for treating members of minority nationalities and races as equal citizens.

In May 1689, five months before the English translation of Locke's *Letter concerning Toleration* would be published, parliament passed the Toleration Act, allowing Protestants who declared their belief in the Trinity to worship openly. However, those who were members of Protestant Churches other than the Church of England continued to be barred from holding civil office.[62] But Locke's letter went much farther than the law, and quickly excited controversy, embrangling Locke in debates with Jonas Proast, chaplain at All Souls College, Oxford, and Henry Stillingfleet, Bishop of Worcester—both opponents of religious toleration, who wrote replies to Locke, provoking subsequent letters from Locke. Already in 1690, Proast published a reply to Locke, who, in turn, responded with *A Second Letter Concerning Toleration*. Proast challenged Locke by insisting that civil government had the obligation to care both for people's welfare in this world and for the salvation of souls and, further, that the government should promote the "true" religion and, if necessary, impose punishments on Dissenters. This punishment, according to Proast, was intended to persuade them to "consider" more carefully the arguments in favor of the Church of England. Proast argued further that religious toleration led directly to moral relativism.[63]

In response, Locke rushed to finish his *Second Letter Concerning Toleration* that same year. Here, he stressed that "If it be true that Magistrates [are] as liable to Error as the rest of Mankind, their using of Force in Matters of Religion, would not at all advance the salvation of Mankind."[64] Accordingly, Locke continued, in a crucial argument, by insisting that "the Magistrate has no Power...to make use of Force in Matters of Religion, for the Salvation of Mens Souls."[65] Proast had held that (Christian) government could *and should* dictate the articles of faith, the form of worship, and all other matters related to what he called the "true" religion. Locke countered:

> ...the Magistrate's Power extends not to the establishing any Articles of Faith, or Forms of Worship, by the force of his Laws. For Laws are of no force at all without Penalties; and Penalties in this case are absolutely impertinent, because they are not proper to convince the Mind.[66]

Moreover, far from achieving their stated purpose to bring Dissenters back into the Church, punishments would more likely provoke resentment on their part and run the risk of inducing those being punished to reject that Church altogether.[67] In consideration of the great diversity of religions in the world, Locke concluded that toleration was the only sensible policy. Proast disputed this and, in his reply to Locke's *Second Letter*, argued that the diversity of faiths was all the more reason for the state to uphold and impose "the *true* Religion."[68]

Locke returned the argument with *A Third Letter for Toleration* (1691), which was almost ten times as long as his original letter. One problem with Proast's recommendation of punishment in order to bring Dissenters back into the "true religion," Locke argued, was that force could not be relied upon to induce more than "an outward Profession of that Religion." But there was no assurance that force could actually suffice to change people's minds about the doctrines of the Church or lead people to give up "their beloved Lusts." On the contrary, people who were persecuted until they consented to profess the established faith might well see "if they can avoid Force, and retain [indulgence in] their Lusts."[69] Locke continued by arguing that

> [s]ince revealed religions are all based upon 'remote matters of fact', we can have only *opinions* about, not knowledge of, their truth... [R]evelation, as it comes to us from Scripture, gives us only an opinion about the truth, not knowledge. [Locke] will argue further than this has political implications: namely, the state's enforcing of religious norms, on the grounds that they are revealed in Scripture, is illegitimate, as this amounts to the state's coercing humans on the basis of mere religious opinion.[70]

That did not settle the matter as far as Proast was concerned and, in 1704, he brought out his *Second Letter to the Author of the Three Letters for Toleration*. Proast now pressed the point that people could feel *persuaded* of the truth of their faith. Locke responded, in *A Fourth Letter for Toleration*, left unfinished at the time of his death in 1704, that feelings were not tantamount to proof or even evidence, and urged that people use their reason to assess the basis for their beliefs. Ultimately, for Locke—as for Immanuel Kant later—it was morality that mattered, and not what individuals made of particular doctrinal claims about the ranks of angels, the number of saints or sacraments, or the nature of the holy trinity. *Natural religion*, by which Locke meant devotion to the principles of morality, was what he considered to be the "one true religion."[71]

In August 1695, Locke published his short book, *The Reasonableness of Christianity*, in which—at a time when the Bishop of Worcester was writing about the centrality of the doctrine of the Trinity—the author said nothing about that doctrine, limiting himself to asserting that to be a Christian was to believe that Jesus of Nazareth was the Christ and that through his death on the cross, he had made salvation possible.[72] But even here he offered a revision of traditional Christianity, by dismissing the notion of original sin, thus concluding that "Christ did not redeem mankind from original sin, but from the loss of immortality that, Locke argued, was the consequence of the Fall."[73] Although he published the book anonymously, his critics quickly guessed his authorship.

Locke's Two Treatises of Government

At one time, Locke's *Second Treatise* was widely treated as a piece of abstract philosophizing, intended to address issues valid in every historical context but not inspired by any particular issues, or—worse—as if the treatises had been written with the American Revolutionaries in mind. When this (mis)interpretation was later debunked, some observers went to the other extreme and began to treat it as akin to Whig propaganda. It is perhaps best, however, to concur with Richard Ashcraft in understanding the *Two Treatises* as reasoned political argument, designed to persuade its readers of certain central points—among them, that the King did not enjoy absolute authority but had to respect the laws of the land and the wishes of the majority as reflected in the deliberations of parliament; and that a King who did not respect these things was, in effect, at war against his own subjects, who might therefore justly remove him from office. The *Treatises* (in particular chapter 5 of the *Second Treatise*) also advanced a justification of English colonization in the New World, as we shall see toward the end of the next section, immediately below.

During the years 1671–1675, Locke served as secretary to the Lords Proprietors of Carolina; in that capacity, he wrote some of the laws governing the colony, including the Temporary Laws of 1674, and collaborated with Shaftesbury in drawing up the Fundamental Constitution of Carolina.[74] But Locke and Shaftesbury were among a minority in England who supported the colonization of America. The majority, including the author of *Britannia Languens*, a tract first published in 1680, held that the plantations being established in the New World were a drain on the English economy.[75] There were also critics who objected that the English had no right to settle on land already inhabited by indigenous peoples. It was, therefore, both to respond to the King's recent challenges to the prerogatives of parliament *and* to defend the colonial project as well as the enclosure movement that, in or around 1679, Locke began writing the text which comprises the *Second Treatise of Government*. That same year, a collection of some of Sir Robert Filmer's writings was published, under the title *The Freeholders' Grand Inquest*. The volume became the center of a lot of debate now; Filmer's position, that monarchy was natural and right, was useful to Charles II, and suggested that Whig demands were unnatural and wrong.

Filmer's *Patriarcha* appeared at the height of the controversy about the King's repeated prorogations of parliament and its publication was clearly intended to strengthen the King's position. But, although Locke objected to Filmer's defense of Scripture-based patriarchy, he would himself be criticized by Mary Astell for preserving certain patriarchal biases (see Box 2.3).

Box 2.3: Mary Astell
Mary Astell (1666–1731), a conservative member of the Church of England, is remembered today for her trenchant criticism of Locke's works, and for pointing out the patriarchal features of his thought. She was a supporter of monarchy and marriage, and an enthusiast for the Stuart dynasty and for Queen Anne (1665–1714; reigned 1702–1714), the last of the Stuart monarchs. Her first published work, *A Serious Proposal to the Ladies for the Advancement of Their True and Greatest Interest*, part 1 (1694) established her reputation—once her authorship was conceded—as a firm champion of the dignity of women and foe of misogyny in all its guises. Her later work, *The Christian Religion as Profess'd by a Daughter of the Church*, published in 1705, was a systematic analysis of several of

---

Locke's works, including his *Essay Concerning Human Understanding*, *The Reasonableness of Christianity*, and *Two Treatises of Government*. She noted that, in the years since 1688, the political position of women had worsened; of symbolic importance was the fact that apologists for the regime of William and Mary emphasized that Queen Mary II had signed over to William III her claim to participate in the rule of England. She further objected to the fact that men had erased the accomplishments of all but the most prominent women from history books, suggesting that— contrary to what the men of her age might wish to suppose—nations flourished the most under female rule; she pointed to England's golden age during the reign of Queen Elizabeth I in support of her contention.

Locke now felt that the refutation he had been drafting was no longer adequate to the task and began writing what is today the *First Treatise*, with extensive quotations from Filmer serving for a point-by-point refutation. This fact, that Locke wrote the *First Treatise* after having largely finished what comprises today the *Second Treatise*, explains why there are references to the *Second Treatise* in many places in the *First*, while there are no references to the *First Treatise* in the *Second*.[76] But, while Locke was working on his refutation of Filmer, Shaftesbury was put on trial for treason; even though he was acquitted, the trial raised tensions between the Tories and the Whigs. At the end of November 1682, as already noted, Shaftesbury fled to Holland. After the beheading of Algernon Sidney a year later, Locke, whose rebuttal of Filmer was, in many regards, similar to or much the same as Sidney's, feared for his life and likewise fled to Holland. Locke asked that his manuscript be sent on after him. It may be that some pages were lost in transit, or it may be that the cautious Locke may have destroyed those portions of his manuscript which he thought royalists would consider the most seditious. Be that as it may, we have Locke's own testimony to the fact that part of the original manuscript no longer exists, for, in the preface to *Two Treatises*, he wrote:

Thou hast here the Beginning and End of a Discourse concerning Government; what Fate has otherwise disposed of the Papers that should have filled up the middle, and were more than all the rest, 'tis not worth while to tell thee.[77]

The *Two Treatises* were finally published in 1690.

In a famous passage in the *Second Treatise*, Locke declared,

...if a long train of Abuses, Prevarications, and Artifices, all tending the same way, make the design visible to the People, and they cannot but feel, what they lie under, and see, whither they are going; 'tis not to be wonder'd, that they should then rouze themselves, and endeavour to put the rule into such hands, which may secure to them the ends for which Government was at first erected...[78]

In the *Two Treatises*, Locke included appeals to the King's own interests, apparently to deflect charges that he was advocating treason and to win over moderates who might fear that the overthrow of another Stuart monarch might return England to the state of civil war from which it had not long before emerged. To succeed, he had to shift the blame for resistance from the Whig Party in parliament to the King and his decrees. This he accomplished, inter alia, by asserting, as already noted, that, insofar as rebellion entails opposition to lawful authority rather than merely to persons, those who violate the laws and act in a way contrary to the constitution were properly called *rebels*. Locke used the same etymological analysis of the word "rebellare" as Sidney had to drive home a different conclusion, viz., that it was the King who was rebelling.[79] He continued by directly addressing the King's repeated prorogations of parliament during the years 1679–1681:

...if any one by force takes away the establish'd Legislative of any Society, and the Laws by them made pursuant to their trust, he thereby takes away the Umpirage, which every one had consented to, for a peaceable decision of all their Controversies, and a bar to the state of War amongst them. They, who remove, or change the Legislative, take away this decisive power, which no Body can have, but by the appointment and consent of the People; and so destroying the Authority...and introducing a Power, which the People hath not authoriz'd, they actually *introduce a state of War*, which is that of Force without Authority: And thus by removing the Legislative establish'd by the Society (in whose decisions the People acquiesced and united, as to that of their own will) they unty the Knot, and *expose the People to anew to the state of War*.[80]

As Nathan Tarcov has explained, by "put[ting] himself 'into a State of War with his People,'" a tyrant brings about "the dissolution of society."[81] The purpose of government, Locke argued, was the preservation of property, and he pointedly noted that he included "Lives, Liberties, and Estates...[under] the general name 'Property'."[82] When the King or government works *against* that purpose and abandons respect for and adherence to the laws of the land, then at that point "Tyranny begins."[83] Locke continued by urging that the legislature is altered "when the King prevents the legislature from meeting or enjoying freedom of debate"[84]— which is exactly what Charles II did by proroguing parliament. Although the King was not rebelling *visibly*, he was engaging in what Locke termed *invisible* rebellion.[85] In such circumstances, "Political power 'devolves to the People, who have a Right to resume their original Liberty.'"[86] In short, "Locke redefines rebellion so that those in power [who violate the laws] rather than those who rightly resist them are guilty of it."[87] Or, as Jonathan Scott has expressed it, "The point of Locke's use of 'rebellare', then, is not to *defend* rebellion, but to redirect the odium involved. The rebel is the monarch, the one who, in circumstances of peace, reintroduces a state of War."[88]

The foundation for Locke's argument, in the *Second Treatise,* was a strong defense of majority rule and rule of law, on the understanding that "*Freedom* then is not what Sir R. F. tells us, *A Liberty for every one to do what he lists, to live as he pleases, and not to be tyed by any Laws:* But *Freedom of Men under Government,* is, to have a standing Rule to live by, common to every one of that Society, and made by the Legislative Power erected in it."[89] Like Algernon Sidney, thus, Locke did *not* equate freedom or liberty with an individual's right to do as he or she pleases— a common contemporary misreading of Locke—but with the rule under laws to which the community has given its consent. Consistently, when it came to individuals, Locke's *Second Treatise* allowed that each person might decide for him- or herself whether the laws seem just, but he made no provision for a right for individuals to resist the government—that was a matter for the people collectively to decide.[90] Thus, although magistrates, like other people, may form their own private opinions about the laws, they must nonetheless obey and execute those laws since the "*Power that every individual gave the Society,* when he entered into it, can never revert to Individuals again, as long as the Society lasts."[91]

Locke on Property

John Locke famously articulated the principle that each individual enjoyed a natural right to "life, liberty, and property," which, in Thomas Jefferson's subsequent translation, would become "life, liberty, and the pursuit of happiness." Locke's defense of this concept of natural rights ("natural rights – notably, rights to life, liberty, and property" which are enjoyed even in the absence of government and which "were retained when men contracted to form political societies" and place themselves under governments[92]) places him within the aforementioned Enlightenment tradition and is, in any event, entailed in his defense of Natural Law. Already in 1646, Leveller Richard Overton (1600?–1660?) had argued (in his *Arrow against all Tyrants*) that every individual had a right to property and that no one had the right to deprive someone of his or her property "without manifest violation and affront to the very principles of nature, and of the Rules of equity and justice...."[93] James Tully explains why the defense of property had become a matter of urgent concern for Locke at the time. As Tully notes, in 1680 the King was claiming the right to levy taxes and confiscate property without parliamentary approval. Filmer's *Patriarcha* was the testament most frequently cited in defense of this policy, because it ascribed to the sovereign superior rights over all the inhabitants of his realm, together with their property.[94] Locke countered this claim on three levels: first, by finding that the parliament, not the King, was the legitimate holder of supreme power; second, by emphasizing the role of positive law in establishing and regulating property in land; and third, by underlining that land use, like political society itself, must serve the public good.[95] In chapter 5 of his *Second Treatise*, one can find Locke's assertions that people have the right to use the earth to their "best advantage...and convenience,"[96] that people establish their property in land through their labor (this figuring as Locke's endorsement of the enclosure movement),[97] that people might accumulate as much as they like, limited only by the provision that they should not destroy the "fruits of the earth" or cause them to spoil or take so much that there does not remain enough for others,[98] and that the invention of money removed the natural limit to the accumulation of wealth, since money does not spoil.[99]

It should be emphasized once again, however, that Locke was addressing the issues of *his* day, *not ours*. Prominent among the issues of his day was the enclosure movement, by which is meant the progressive fencing off (or enclosing) of tracts of land as private property, thereby eliminating common lands hitherto available for grazing. Enclosures during Tudor times resulted in the destruction of villages, and agrarian revolts against enclosures swept over the country in the mid-sixteenth century, during the reign of Edward VI.

But property was a hot issue not only in England, in Locke's day, but also in the New World, where English colonists had been settling since the beginning of the seventeenth century. Thus, Locke's theory of property was also tailored to address the question of whether the colonists from England had any business treating the New World as vacant land. In addition to defending the thesis that the plantations were economically profitable for English interests, Locke spelled out three main arguments in justification of colonization and the establishment of colonial ownership of land already inhabited by local peoples, supplementing these with two further arguments. *First*, drawing upon Father Joseph d'Acosta's travelogue of the West Indies (published in 1604) but ignoring the clergyman's repeated allusions to the nationhood established by the indigenous nations, Locke contended on the contrary that the indigenous peoples lived in a "state of nature" with neither government nor laws of any kind to regulate them.[100] Insofar as he held that "in Governments the Laws regulate the right of property, and the possession of land is determined by positive constitutions,"[101] it followed, in his view, that indigenous people's possession of their land was not protected by law. Accordingly, anyone who settled on land in the New World and worked it was entitled to claim it as his property.[102] *Second*, Locke defined labor as agricultural cultivation, which he considered "the only rational justification for property in products of the earth."[103] In order to make this second argument work in favor of the colonists, however, Locke had to disregard the fact that many indigenous people were, in fact, tilling the soil. Thus, *third*, ignoring William Wood's *New Englands Prospectus* (1634), in which the author noted that the indigenous people with whom he was familiar had not only mastered farming techniques but had even instructed the colonists on how to plant corn, Locke instead characterized the indigenous people as hunters and gatherers, but not farmers, and, on that fallacious foundation, advanced the problematic proposition that those prepared to farm the land (the English, as far as Locke was concerned) were in their right to enclose the land, thus depriving the those already living there of any claim to what had been theirs.[104]

The foregoing three arguments sufficed for Locke to declare that English colonists had the *right* to take possession of land in the New World. But he developed a *fourth* argument, designed to suggest that there might be something akin to a *duty* to do so. This fourth argument consisted of two points, of which the first consisted of the allegation that "Land that is left wholly to Nature, that hath no improvement of

Pasturage, Tillage, or Planting, is called, as indeed it is, *wast[e];* and we shall find the benefit of it amount to little more than nothing."[105] The second point, complementing the first, is that not only would the indigenous people not be injured in any way by English plantations, but they would actually stand to benefit from them![106] And *finally*, Locke held out the prospect that the indigenous people, if they converted to Christianity, adopted English ways, and accepted English laws, could enjoy the same rights as the English settlers.[107]

Locke on Slavery

Locke, together with Ashley/Shaftesbury, had invested in the Royal African Company, which was involved in the slave trade, and in the Bahamas Adventurers company, which was involved in the plantations in the Bahamas, plantations being worked by African slaves. Locke participated in drafting the charter for the Carolina colony. The charter included the clause, "every freeman of Carolina shall have absolute power and authority over his negro slaves."[108] Locke even served as a Sub-Governor of the Royal African Company until 1673.[109] Later, Locke took part in drawing up Instructions to the Governor of Virginia in 1698, describing the slaves as "justifiably enslaved" on the argument that they had been taken into custody in a "just war."[110] There is no dispute that Locke was well informed about colonial slavery and that he benefitted financially from the slave trade. Interestingly, as Nancy Morrow has pointed out, Locke gave no indication of being aware that there could be any conflict between his advocacy of political liberty (in practice, for male landowners) and his defense of slavery.[111] What is in dispute is whether his comments on slavery were intended in any way to justify the enslavement of Africans.

Certainly, in Locke's view, the peoples of sub-Saharan Africa were living in a state of nature.[112] Yet his comments about slavery in *Two Treatises* point in different directions. On the one hand, he began the *First Treatise* by declaring that

> Slavery is so vile and miserable an Estate of Man, and so directly opposite to the generous Temper and Courage of our Nation; that 'tis hardly to be conceived, that an *Englishman*, much less a *Gentleman*, should plead for't.[113]

On the other hand, even while declaring that every person was born free, Locke nonetheless allowed that persons taken captive in a just war might legitimately be enslaved (although children born to slaves were, in his opinion, born free).[114] Locke's ideas about property were relevant both for the English enclosure movement and for the New World, though it does not seem that his comments on slavery were directed toward addressing the African slave trade. On the contrary, his concerns were with refuting Filmer's claim that all people are born slaves and with advancing the proposition that

> ...whenever the Legislators endeavour to take away, and destroy the Property of the People, or to reduce them under Arbitrary Power, they put themselves into a state of War with the People, who are thereupon absolved from any farther Obedience.[115]

Locke's concern, in other words, was with the danger of an English King reducing the *English* people to slavery—which, in turn, justified resistance, in Locke's view. As for the enslavement of Africans, Locke confined his comments to reporting facts and did not endeavor to justify it.

2.4   THE IMPORTANCE OF ALGERNON SIDNEY AND JOHN LOCKE

The ideas of Sidney and Locke seem mainstream today. But in their day, their appeal to reason and demand for a greater measure of freedom for "God-fearing" citizens was radical. So too was their opposition to absolute monarchy and its supposed justification by appeal to the so-called divine right of kings, as well as Locke's articulate defense of a reasonably expansive religious liberty. And again, they were radical in demanding recognition of rights to life, liberty (including, within certain limits, freedom of conscience), and property. Reason was usually defended by them under the terms *Universal Reason* (meaning what all rational people could understand, especially where morality was concerned) and *Natural Law* (here, specifically the moral law). Their writings were read in America and had a direct influence on developments there, as well as in France. Indeed, a portion of Locke's *Second Treatise* was published anonymously in French translation in 1691, and the entire *Second Treatise* was published in Boston in 1773, just as tempers in Britain's colonies in North America were heating up.[116] Finally, both Sidney and Locke helped to shape the political assumptions which are widespread in the West today (and perhaps especially in the United States), so that Edward Feser could write (in 2007), that the world in which we live is "to a very great extent a Lockean world."[117]

NOTES

1. Here I am following Jonathan Scott, *Algernon Sidney and the Restoration Crisis, 1677–1683* (Cambridge: Cambridge University Press, 1991) [hereafter, *Algernon Sidney, 1677–1683*], pp. 261–264. By contrast with Scott's account, Alan Houston writes that not only Locke but also Sidney thought that a magistrate who acted outside the law could be fairly characterized as a "rebel." Since both Scott and Houston ground their interpretations in extracts from Sidney's *Discourses*, I suggest that the discrepancy reflects inconsistencies in Sidney's work, due to the fact that he was executed before he could finalize it for publication. See Alan Craig Houston, *Algernon Sidney and the Republican Heritage in England and America* (Princeton, N.J.: Princeton University Press, 1991), p. 213.
2. As quoted in Blair Worden, "The Commonwealth Kidney of Algernon Sidney", in *Journal of British Studies*, Vol. 24, No. 1 (January 1985), p. 2.
3. As quoted in Caroline Robbins, "Algernon Sidney's Discourses Concerning Government: Textbook of Revolution", in *The William and Mary Quarterly*, 3rd Ser., Vol. 4, No. 3 (July 1947), p. 269.
4. Mark Knights, "Petitioning and the Political Theorists: John Locke, Algernon Sidney and London's 'Monster' Petition of 1680", in *Past and Present*, No. 138 (February 1993), p. 106.
5. As quoted in Blair Worden, *Roundhead Reputations: The English Civil Wars and the Passions of Posterity: The English Civil War and the Passions of Posterity* (London: Allen Lane, 2001), p. 129.
6. Sidney had in fact been conspiring with Lord Russell, the Duke of Monmouth, the Earl of Essex, and others with the objective of enlisting the Scots to stage a rebellion, in order to create a situation in which the King might be removed from power. See Richard Ashcraft, *Revolutionary Politics & Locke's Two Treatises of Government* (Princeton, N.J.: Princeton University Press,

1986), pp. 363–371. For some of the complexities surrounding the Rye House Plot, see also Houston, *Algernon Sidney and the Republican Heritage*, pp. 59–61.

7. Worden, *Roundhead Reputations*, p. 130.

8. Scott, *Algernon Sidney, 1677–1683*, p. 319.

9. As quoted in *Ibid.*, p. 329. For the record of the trial, see *The arraignment, tryal & condemnation of Algernon Sidney, Esq. for high treason...before the Right Honourable Sir George Jeffreys...Lord Chief Justice of England at His Majesties Court of Kingsbench at Westminster on the 7th, 21th [sic] and 27th of November, 1683* (London: B. Tooke, 1684), downloaded from Northwestern University Library, Evanston, Illinois.

10. *Colonel Sidney's Speech, Delivered to the Sheriff On the Scaffolrd, December 7th 1683* (London: N.P., 1683), pp. 4, 5, downloaded from Northwestern University Library, Evanston, Illinois.

11. As quoted in John Locke, *Two Treatises of Government*, ed. by Peter Laslett (Cambridge: Cambridge University Press, 1988), *First Treatise*, Book I, para. 5, p. 143.

12. Scott, *Algernon Sidney, 1677–1683*, p. 195.

13. Benedetto Fontana, "Love of Country and Love of God: The Political Uses of Religion in Machiavelli", in *Journal of the History of Ideas*, Vol. 60, No. 4 (1999), pp. 652–655.

14. Niccolò Machiavelli, *The Prince*, trans. from Italian by Russell Price, ed. by Quentin Skinner (Cambridge: Cambridge University Press, 1988), chapter IX, p. 35.

15. "Niccolò Machiavelli", in *Stanford Encyclopedia of Philosophy*, first published 13 September 2005, Copyright © 2005 by Cary Nederman, at plato.stanford.edu/entries/machiavelli/ [accessed on 7 January 2024], p. 7 of 15.

16. "Hugo Grotius", in *Stanford Encyclopedia of Philosophy*, first published 16 December 2005; substantive revision 8 January 2021, Copyright © 2021 by Jon Miller, at https://plato.stanford.edu/entries/grotius/#NatuLaw [accessed on 4 January 2024].

17. Scott, *Algernon Sidney*, p. 217.

18. Algernon Sidney, *Discourses Concerning Government*, Third edition (London: Printed for A. Millar, 1751), *Eighteenth Century Collections Online*, at Northwestern University Library [this and all other citations from *Discourses* were accessed on 7 January 2011], chap. 2, section 3, p. 70.

19. *Ibid.*, chap. 1, section 2, p. 6.
20. *Ibid.*, chap. 1, section 2, p. 7.
21. *Ibid.*, chap. 1, section 16, p. 38.
22. *Ibid.*, chap. 3, section 41, pp. 437–438.
23. Scott, *Algernon Sidney, 1677–1683*, p. 230.
24. Jonathon Scott, *Algernon Sidney and the English Republic, 1623–1677* (Cambridge: Cambridge University Press, 1988) [hereafter, *Algernon Sidney, 1623–1677*], p. 4.
25. Sidney, *Discourses*, chap. 3, section 13, p. 307 and chap. 3, section 17, p. 323.
26. *Ibid.*, chap. 3, section 17, p. 323.
27. Scott, *Algernon Sidney, 1623–1677*, p. 137; confirmed in Houston, *Algernon Sidney and the Republic Heritage*, p. 175.
28. Melissa A. Butler, "Early Liberal Roots of Feminism: John Locke's Attack on Patriarchy", in Nancy J. Hirschmann and Kirstie M. McClure (eds.), *Feminist Interpretations of John Locke* (University Park, PA: The Pennsylvania State University Press, 2007), p. 98.
29. Houston, *Algernon Sidney and the Republic Heritage*, p. 179.
30. Sidney, *Discourses*, chap. 2, section 6, and chap. 3, sections 19, 31, 36, 38, and 41.
31. *Ibid.*, chap. 2, section 24, pp. 172 and 181.
32. Worden, *Roundhead Reputations*, pp. 164–165. See Algernon Sidney, *Court Maxims*, ed. by Hans W. Blom, Eco Haitsma Mulier, and Ronald Janse (Cambridge: Cambridge University Press, 1996).
33. Ashcraft, *Revolutionary Politics*, pp. 370–379; and Houston, *Algernon Sidney and the Republican Heritage*, pp. 59–61.
34. Ashcraft, *Revolutionary Politics*, p. 410.
35. Maurice Cranston, *John Locke: A Biography* (London and New York: Longmans, Green & Co., 1957), chap. 2 (pp. 18–28).
36. *Ibid.*, p. 41.
37. *Ibid.*, pp. 93–95, 113.
38. Concerning Locke's years in Amsterdam, see *ibid.*, chap. 17 (pp. 231—238).
39. John Locke, *An Essay Concerning Human Understanding*, Complete and unabridged, collated and annotated by Alexander Campbell Fraser (New York: Dover Publications, 1959), vol. 1 (535 pp.) and vol. 2 (495 pp.).

40. Edward Feser, *Locke* (Oxford: Oneworld, 2007), p. 33.
41. Marc D. Hauser, *Moral Minds: How nature designed our universal sense of right and wrong* (New York: Ecco Books, 2006).
42. Roger Woolhouse, "Locke's theory of knowledge", in Vere Chappell (ed.), *The Cambridge Companion to Locke* (Cambridge: Cambridge University Press, 1994; reprinted 2006), p. 151.
43. Locke, *An Essay Concerning Human Understanding*, Book IV, chap. IV, p. 232.
44. Locke, *Second Treatise*, chap. 9, para. 124, p. 351.
45. Locke, *An Essay Concerning Human Understanding*, Book IV, chap. III, p. 208.
46. *Ibid.*, Book IV, chap. III, p. 195.
47. Feser, *Locke*, p. 110, quoting from *Essay*. On this point, see also James Tully, *A Discourse on Property: John Locke and His adversaries* (Cambridge: Cambridge University Press, 1980), p. 101.
48. Roger Woolhouse, *Locke: A Biography* (Cambridge: Cambridge UniversityPress, 2007), p. 31.
49. As quoted in *Ibid.*, p. 40.
50. As quoted in Geraint Parry, *John Locke* (London: George Allen & Unwin, 1978), p. 83.
51. As quoted in Woolhouse, *Locke*, p. 42.
52. Richard Vernon, *The Career of Toleration: John Locke, Jonas Proast, and After* (Montreal and New York: McGill-Queen's University Press, 1997), p. 25.
53. Robert P. Kraynak, "John Locke: From Absolutism to Toleration", in *American Political Science Review*, Vol. 74, Issue 1 (March 1980), p. 55.
54. As quoted in *ibid.*, p. 55.
55. W. M. Spellman, *John Locke* (New York: St. Martin's Press, 1997), p. 16.
56. For discussion of the *Essay on Toleration*, see John Dunn, *The Political Thought of John Locke: An Historical Account of the Argument of the 'Two Treatises of Government'* (Cambridge: Cambridge University Press, 1969), chap. 4.
57. John Locke, *A Letter Concerning Toleration*, trans. from Latin by William Popple (Amherst, N.Y.: Prometheus Books, 1990), p. 31.
58. *Ibid.*, p. 18.
59. *Ibid.*, p. 61.
60. *Ibid.*, pp. 69–70.

61. Ashcraft, *Revolutionary Politics*, p. 100.
62. Vernon, *The Career of Toleration*, p. 7.
63. See Adam Wolfston, "Toleration and Relativism: The Locke-Proast Exchange", in *The Review of Politics*, Vol. 59, No. 2 (Spring 1997), especially pp. 215–217.
64. John Locke, *A Second Letter concerning Toleration* (London: Printed for Awnsham and John Churchill, 1690), posted at https://quod.lib.umich.edu/e/eebo/A48891.0001.001?view=fulltext [accessed on 24 June 2023], p. 6.
65. *Ibid.*, p. 6.
66. *Ibid.*, p. 7.
67. *Ibid.*, pp. 9, 15.
68. Jonas Proast, *A Third Letter Concerning Toleration* (1691), as summarized in Wolfson, "Toleration and Relativism", p. 217.
69. John Locke, *A Third Letter for Toleration* (London: Printed for Awnsham and John Churchill, 1692), at https://quod.lib.umich.edu/e/eebo/A489000.001.001?view=fulltext [accessed on 24 June 2023], pp. 157, 159.
70. Wolfson, "Toleration and Relativism", pp. 218–219.
71. *Ibid.*, p. 224.
72. Nicholas Wolterstoff, "Locke's Philosophy of Religion", in Chappell (ed.), *The Cambridge Companion to Locke*, p. 185; and J. B. Schneewind, "Locke's Moral Philosophy", in *Ibid.*, p. 217.
73. Hans Aarsleff, "Locke's Influence", in Chappell (ed.), *The Cambridge Companion to Locke*, p. 257.
74. Barbara Arneil, "Trade, Plantations, and Property: John Locke and the Economic Defense of Colonialism", in *Journal of the History of Ideas*, Vol. 55, No. 4 (October 1994), p. 592.
75. *Ibid.*, pp. 593–597.
76. I am following Peter Laslett's interpretation here.
77. Locke, *Two Treatises*, preface, p. 137.
78. *Ibid.*, *Second Treatise*, para. 225, p. 415.
79. *Ibid.*, *Second Treatise*, para. 226, pp. 415–416.
80. *Ibid.*, *Second Treatise*, para. 227, p. 416 (Locke's emphasis).
81. Nathan Tarcov, "Locke's *Second Treatise* and 'The Best Fence Against Rebellion'", in *The Review of Politics*, Vol. 43, No. 2 (April 1981), pp. 206, 212.
82. Locke, *Second Treatise*, chap. 9, para. 124 and 123, pp. 350–351.
83. *Ibid.*, chap. 19, para. 202, p. 400.

84. Tarcov, "Locke's *Second Treatise*", p. 208.
85. *Ibid.*
86. *Ibid.*, p. 210, quoting from Locke, *Second Treatise*, para. 212.
87. Tarcov, "Locke's *Second Treatise*", p. 212.
88. Jonathan Scott, "The Law of War: Grotius, Sidney, Locke and the Political Theory of Rebellion", in *History of Political Thought*, Vol. 13, No. 4 (Winter 1992), p. 582.
89. Locke, *Second Treatise*, para. 22, pp. 283–284, emphasis as given.
90. Jacqueline Stevens, "The Reasonableness of John Locke's Majority: Property Rights, Consent, and Resistance in the Second Treatise", in *Political Theory*, Vol. 24, No. 3 (August 1996), p. 443.
91. Locke, *Second Treatise*, para. 243, pp. 427–428, emphasis as given.
92. Maurice Cranston, "Locke and Liberty", in *The Wilson Quarterly*, Vol. 10, No. 5 (Winter 1986), p. 87.
93. As quoted in J. P. Day, "Locke on Property", in *History of Philosophy*, Vol. 16, Issue 64 (July 1966), p. 219.
94. Tully, *A Discourse on Property*, p. 172.
95. *Ibid.*, pp. 122–123, 160, 162.
96. Locke, *Second Treatise*, para. 26, p. 286.
97. *Ibid.*, para. 27, p. 288.
98. *Ibid.*, para. 31, p. 290.
99. *Ibid.*, para. 36, p. 293.
100. Barbara Arneil, *John Locke and America: The Defence of English Colonialism* (Oxford: Clarendon Press, 1996; reprinted, 1998), pp. 38–39.
101. Locke, *Second Treatise*, para. 50, p. 344.
102. *Ibid.*, para. 27, pp. 328–329. See also Michael Witgen, "A Nation of Settlers: The Early American Republic and the Colonization of the Northwest Territory", in *The William and Mary Quarterly*, Vol. 76, No. 3 (July 2019), pp. 391–392.
103. Arneil, *John Locke and America*, p. 137; confirmed in Tully, *A Discourse on Property*, pp. 122–123.
104. Arneil, *John Locke and America*, pp. 41, 139, and passim; and Jennifer Welchman, "Locke on Slavery and Inalienable Rights", in *Canadian Journal of Philosophy*, Vol. 25, No. 1 (March 1995), p. 78.
105. Locke, *Second Treatise*, para. 42, p. 339, Locke's emphasis.

106. *Ibid.*, para. 37, p. 336; and Arneil, *John Locke and America*, pp. 150–152.
107. See Arneil, *John Locke and America*, pp. 127, 134, and especially 166.
108. As quoted in Nancy V. Morrow, "The Problem of Slavery in the Polemic Literature of the American Enlightenment", in *Early American Literature*, Vol. 20, No. 3 (Winter 1985/1986), p. 237.
109. Welchman, "Locke on Slavery", p. 73; James Farr, "Locke, Natural Law, and New World Slavery", in *Political Theory*, Vol. 36, No. 4 (August 2008), p. 497; and Wayne Glausser, "Three Approaches to Locke and the Slave Trade", in *Journal of the History of Ideas*, Vol. 51, No. 2 (April–June 1990), p. 201.
110. Morrow, "The Problem of Slavery", p. 237.
111. *Ibid.*, p. 237.
112. Welchman, "Locke on Slavery", p. 78. That Locke intended for his allusions to the state of nature to be taken literally is clear from *Second Treatise*, para. 101, p. 178.
113. Locke, *First Treatise*, para. 1, p. 175, emphasis as given.
114. Locke, *Second Treatise*, para. 187–190, pp. 440–441.
115. *Ibid.*, para. 222, p. 460, emphasis removed.
116. Terrell Carver, "Gender and Narrative in Locke's *Two Treatises of Government*", in Hirschmann and McClure (eds.), *Feminist Interpretations of John Locke*, p. 192.
117. Feser, *Locke*, p. 1.

FURTHER READINGS

Arneil, Barbara. *John Locke and America: The Defence of English Colonialism* (Clarendon Press, 1996).
———. "Trade, Plantations, and Property: John Locke and the Economic Defense of Colonialism", in *Journal of the History of Ideas*, Vol. 55, No. 4 (October 1994).
Ashcraft, Richard. *Revolutionary Politics & Locke's Two Treatises of Government* (Princeton University Press, 1986).
Dunn, John. *The Political Thought of John Locke: An Historical Account of the Argument of "Two Treatises of Government"* (Cambridge University Press, 1969).

Houston, Alan Craig. *Algernon Sidney and the Republican Heritage in England and America* (Princeton University Press, 1991).

Robbins, Caroline. "Algernon Sidney's Discourses Concerning Government: Textbook of Revolution", in *The William and Mary Quarterly*, 3rd Ser., Vol. 4, No. 3 (July 1947).

Sapiro, Virgiinia. *A Vindication of Political Virtue: The Political Theory of Mary Wollstonecraft* (Chicago: University of Chicago Press, 1992).

Scott, Jonathan. *Algernon Sidney and the English Republic, 1623–1677* (Cambridge University Press, 1988).

———. *Algernon Sidney and the Restoration Crisis, 1677–1683* (Cambridge University Press, 1991).

Spellman, *John Locke* (St. Martin's Press, 1997).

Taylor, Barbara. *Mary Wollstonecraft and the Feminist Imagination* (Cambridge University Press, 2003).

Wardle, Ralph M. *Mary Wollstonecraft: A Critical Biography* (London & Lawrence, KS: The Richards Press & the University of Kansas Press, 1951).

CHAPTER 3

The Scottish Enlightenment: Francis Hutcheson, David Hume, and Adam Smith

Torbjørn L. Knutsen

Abstract During the eighteenth-century Scotland emerged as a leading force of Enlightenment ideas. Three of its most famous Scottish representatives were Francis Hutcheson, David Hume, and Adam Smith. None of them were political philosophers in the traditional sense of the term, yet all made lasting contributions to political thought—Hutcheson by laying the conceptual groundwork for a new science of moral philosophy; Hume by criticizing the established views of social-contract theory and the verities of trade and economic transactions; Smith by developing an influential theory of the self-regulating market and pioneering the field of political economy.

Keywords Calvinism · Science · Secular thought · Moral philosophy · Act of Union · Sense of beauty · Honor · Sense of the ridiculous · Skepticism · Social contract · God & evil

Seventeenth-century Scotland was a deeply religious society, located in the Atlantic periphery of Europe. It was one of the poorest countries in Europe, and Edinburgh was a dour near-theocracy, gripped by rigid

© The Author(s), under exclusive license to Springer Nature Switzerland AG 2024
S. P. Ramet and T. L. Knutsen, *Key Thinkers of the English, Scottish and American Enlightenments*,
https://doi.org/10.1007/978-3-031-62454-4_3

and intolerant Calvinism. During the early decades of the 1700s, Scotland was swept by the early winds of the Enlightenment which ushered in economic development and a new intellectual climate. The country emerged as a leader of science and secular thought. Scotland prospered. Edinburgh became a cosmopolitan center of thought. Thinkers like Francis Hutcheson, Adam Ferguson, David Hume, William Robertson, Adam Smith, and others were at the cutting edge of social thought and would help convert the "Moral Philosophy" of the eighteenth century into what would become the disciplines of economics, history, and sociology of the nineteenth.

The rapid secularization that swept early eighteenth-century Scotland did not mean full secularization. Religious sentiments still had deep roots in society. The Christian faith is clearly echoed in the Moral Philosophy of Francis Hutcheson, whose lectures on ethics included a discussion of "Our duties towards God."[1] David Hume, by contrast, was critical of religion. His views stirred deep controversies and undermined his employment opportunities.[2] Hume worked many jobs to make ends meet—as librarian, secretary, military officer, and diplomat—and never landed a teaching job. Despite his fame as one of the major thinkers on the British Isles, his applications for professorships were repeatedly turned down because of his radical views on religion.

Adam Smith kept his religious views to himself and taught at the University of Glasgow for several years, succeeding Hutcheson in the Chair of Moral Philosophy there. Hutcheson, Hume, and Smith are famous representatives of the Scottish Enlightenment. Hume and Smith were good friends. They were, like other eighteenth-century thinkers, affected by the English Enlightenment, especially by leading lights such as Locke and Newton. In addition, they were influenced by French *philosophes*—Hume in particular. He lived in France in a formative period of his life, kept in touch with the French academic scene, and gained a large following in France. He admired Rousseau—and even brought him to England in 1766, in a vain attempt to rescue him from persecution. Smith's writings carry echoes of Rousseau and, after his tour of France in the mid-1760s, of the French economists, especially Quesnay.

Hutcheson is often seen as the "father" of the Scottish Enlightenment, with Hume and Smith as his two most brilliant students. Hutcheson defined what would become their common ambition, viz., to develop a science that could detect patterns and regularities in society, and produce useful knowledge on which governments and legislators could draw to improve the order and the welfare of the nation. Hutcheson was a systems-builder—synthesizing his views in a three-volume work with the telling title *A System of Moral Philosophy*. Smith formulated his views in two volumes—*The Theory of Moral Sentiments* and *The Wealth of Nations* which together spelled out his system of Moral Philosophy. Hutcheson and Smith embraced the overall Enlightenment concerns of Reason, Rights, and Progress. Hume did not express his views in a big, synthetic work; his contributions to political theory were instead scattered among a score or so of learned essays. He was a skeptic. And if he built a system, it was in the field of philosophy of knowledge. His first book in this field, *Treatise of Human Nature*, has emerged over time as one of his most frequently read works.

All three authors shared the idea that human beings interrelate and that they, through their incessant interaction, constitute social systems. As they discussed Moral Philosophy, they did so with more than a nod to Isaac Newton, the most celebrated scientist of the age. They all had studied Newton's work. They admired it deeply and they sought to emulate its logical structure and import this into their own philosophical systems.

The intellectual transformation that gripped Scotland during the first half of the eighteenth century was extraordinary and is famously known as the "Scottish Enlightenment."[3]

This chapter will first outline the moral philosophy of Francis Hutcheson and then discuss the political and social ideas of two of his most gifted students: David Hume and Adam Smith—perhaps the two most famous Scottish thinkers of the age. All three were preoccupied with the relations between rational and free individuals and the society of which they were a part. Is there a cohesive force that binds individual humans together? And if there is some kind of cohesive force, can individuals be free and at the same time be members of an orderly society that imposes a restraint on their liberties? Hutcheson, Hume, and Smith all addressed questions like this—and they answered them by postulating the existence of a unifying moral force. However, before presenting the three thinkers, it is useful to comment briefly on the time and place in which they lived and whose society they there investigated.

3.1   THE NATURE AND SETTING
OF THE SCOTTISH ENLIGHTENMENT

The Enlightenment is often associated with the advent of new ideas. These ideas were implemented and affected changes in agriculture, manufacture, exchange, and politics. Most regions in Europe were affected by these changes—Italy, France, Spain, and other places had Enlightenments. But Scotland was special. Nowhere was the transformation as fast and deep as here.

One reason for this was that social and political reforms shook Scotland around 1700. One of the most important of these occurred in 1707, when the Parliaments of England and Scotland combined to form Great Britain. This so-called Act of Union provoked angry reactions from established and privileged members of society. A common opposition to Britain undoubtedly altered the pitch of Scottish politics and increased the solidarity of the nation. The reforms also presented opportunities, e.g., to traders and shippers who were now included in the growing system of trade in the British colonies and who could reap the benefits of commerce. This was not lost on David Hume and Adam Smith, who observed the rapid growth in commerce and associated it with the benefits of free trade.

There is, however, little doubt that transformations were rapid because new ideas struck roots in Scottish society. One feature that made Scottish society particularly receptive to these ideas was the frugal and pragmatic attitude of the people. The Scots followed the debates in England and the Continent. They were early students of Isaac Newton and John Locke, but they read them with a pragmatic eye to how they could use the new ideas for practical purposes. When they saw that the new ideas promised improvements in everyday life, did they introduce them to the Scottish universities.

A second predisposition was the tight-knit and gregarious nature of Scotland's academic community. In other places such communities could be quarrelsome and conflictual, but Scottish academics stressed the virtues of solidarity and cooperation. Where France had aristocratic salons, Scotland had pubs, clubs, and coffee houses. Scientific societies emerged in the towns of the four ancient universities of Glasgow, Aberdeen, St Andrews, and Edinburgh like mushrooms after rain. Here Enlightenment ideas were not exploited to taunt religious sentiments and undermine the congenital atmosphere. In contrast to Paris, where new ideas often sparked abstract quarrels and academic one-upmanship, Scotland provided a more amiable and cooperative environment. New ideas were discussed in a pragmatic spirit. And the discussions suited Scotland's religious tenor well. Newton's calculations of the heavenly bodies were not seen as a challenge to God; rather they were seen as confirming His wisdom and omnipotence. Thus, by the threshold of the eighteenth century, Scottish academics were studying Newton's *Principia Mathematica* (1687) with reverence. And they were reading Locke's *Two Treatises of Government* (1689) and his *Essay Concerning Human Understanding* (1690) with an eye toward how they could improve education and research.

The effects of the new ideas were startling. During the course of the 1700s, Scotland emerged as one of Europe's major centers of learning. An English visitor to Edinburgh in the early 1770s wrote: "Here I stand at what is called the cross of Edinburgh, and can, in a few minutes, take 50 men of genius and learning by the hand."[4] Among the men he might chance to meet was Adam Ferguson who was writing down his observations of the changing society around him in ways that would produce classics in sociology. William Robertson was also preoccupied with social change, and his discussions altered the discipline of History. James Hutton was at the cutting edge of what would later become the field of geology. The English visitor might also chance to meet David Hume and Adam Smith, both good friends of Hutton, both of them analyzing the processes of production and trade, paving the way for the modern science of economics.

3.2   FRANCIS HUTCHESON

One of the most important of the Scottish philosophers was Francis Hutcheson (1694–1746). He was of Irish stock—born in Ulster, the son of a Presbyterian minister. In 1710, he went to Glasgow to study theology, philosophy, and classics. He concluded his studies in 1716 and was licensed as a minister of the Church of Scotland. But he failed to get a job. His Irish roots and his association with dissenting theologians hurt his chances of employment in Scotland. In 1718, he returned to Ireland where he taught for 11 years.

Hutcheson's Contributions

Upon his return to Ireland, Hutcheson established an academy in Dublin. He taught while studying philosophy on the side. He also wrote several essays which he published anonymously. The most famous of them is *An Inquiry into the Original of our Ideas of Beauty and Virtue* (1725), which had as its vantage point the famous axiom of Locke's philosophy of knowledge, viz., that all human knowledge is acquired through sense experience. Hutcheson agreed with Locke that humans acquire experience through the senses of sight, hearing, touch, taste, and smell. But then added that in addition to these five external senses, humans also have several internal senses; among these are the senses of beauty and of morality.

Hutcheson tried to clarify his argument in *An Essay on the Nature and Conduct on the Passions and Affections, with Illustrations upon the Moral Sense* (1728). Here he argued that in addition to the five external senses, humans also have four internal ones. There included the senses of beauty, of honor, and of the ridiculous; and then there was the most important sense of them all: what Hutcheson called "the moral sense." This was a uniquely important sense because it provided a key solidaric principle of human society. This moral sense was implanted in humankind. It pronounces instinctively and immediately on the character of actions and affections, approving those that are virtuous and disapproving those that are vicious. The fact that each and every human being is endowed with moral sense contributes greatly to holding society together.

In 1729, Hutcheson returned to Glasgow, where he succeeded his old master, Gershom Carmichael, as the Chair of Moral Philosophy. His inaugural lecture, which discussed the natural fellowship of mankind, relied on his philosophy of moral sentiment.

Hutcheson did not contribute greatly to advance the field of philosophy while at Glasgow. His most famous writings were behind him. He now devoted himself to teaching—and did so with great success. He divided the subject of Moral Philosophy into four parts: ethics, jurisprudence, economics, and politics.[5]

Hutcheson insisted that humans were social beings. His posthumously published *System of Moral Philosophy* (1755) argued that solitary human beings cannot survive for long; and that a man alone can "scarcely procure to himself the bare necessities of life." Human beings need society. Society means cooperation and individual humans need to cooperate to survive.

It is well known, argues Hutcheson, that in society a man can specialize in a particular sort of work; he will thereby "soon acquire skill and dexterity" and increase his productivity. And if many men specialize in a similar manner—"one grows expert in tillage, another in pasture and breeding cattle, a third in masonry, a fourth in the chaser, a fifth in iron-works, a sixth in the arts of the loom"—then each specialized man will produce a quantity of goods of one kind; some of these he can, in turn, exchange for goods that are produced by other specialized men. Thus, each man will be well off. And society as a whole will increase in wealth.[6]

Critics and Disciples

Hutcheson was popular with students. They were drawn to his classes by his eloquence and his sharp and, at times, controversial wit. His faith in God was unshakable. Yet, his views were radical for his day and attracted criticism. Among his sternest critics were the religious authorities of Glasgow. Secular writers, too, begged to differ with Hutcheson's views—especially his views of Moral Philosophy.

Critics. In 1738 the Presbyterian community of the city rose up in criticism against him. They protested his natural theory of moral sentiments and argued that people cannot have a knowledge of good and evil before they have a knowledge of God. More secular thinkers criticized him for different reasons. Adherents of Thomas Hobbes disagreed with Hutcheson's claim that solitary men would not survive for very long; their entire social-contract theory hinged on the vision of solitary individuals existing in a pre-social state of nature. Adherents of John Locke disagreed with the idea that human beings possessed an innate moral sentiment; they did not dispute the social nature of man but argued that it was an outcome of reason alone.

Adam Ferguson (1723–1816) levied another objection against Hutcheson. Ferguson, professor of Natural Philosophy at the University of Edinburgh, rejected the idea that human beings were endowed with innate and natural moral sentiments. He argued instead that all human properties are the result of historical evolution. Nature has not equipped human beings with an innate moral sense, he argued; humans have instead developed moral attitudes during the course of their social interaction, he maintained. He sought to substantiate his claim in his *Essay on the History of Civil Society* (1767).

Hutcheson, Ferguson, and the Glasgow presbytery did not agree on the nature of man; however, they agreed on one thing: that humans were sociable beings. This agreement was widely embraced by other Scottish thinkers as well. But where did that sociability come from? This question was intensely debated by the academic elite of late eighteenth-century

Scotland. And it received several answers. Some of them by Hutcheson's own students.

Disciples. Two important disciples were David Hume (1711–1776) and Adam Smith (1723–1790). Both were deeply affected by Hutcheson's Moral Philosophy and by the English thinkers he invoked—among them Newton and Locke. But they were also influenced by the thinkers of the French Enlightenment. Like many other Scottish thinkers of the day, they cultivated close relations with France. Hume and Smith admired Montesquieu and Voltaire. Hume had a high opinion of Rousseau. Smith was deeply influenced by the French economist François Quesnay (1694–1774).

Neither Hume nor Smith were political philosophers in the traditional sense of the term. Hume wrote books on perception and understanding, but he wrote no single, synthesising work on political philosophy. His political writings are scattered across a large number of essays. Smith, by contrast, developed an impressive philosophical system. However, he did not direct his attention toward politics; instead, he directed his main attention toward the economic aspects of Moral Philosophy.

Hume and Smith were the best of friends. They read Newton and Locke. And they read each other. They shared a philosophy of knowledge which portrayed science as a journey of discovery—a process that evolved from wonder to admiration as our imagination established increasing links and connections among disorderly events. They both admired Newton and noted how he described the solar system as a dynamic unity, where the planets are held in place by gravitational forces. Both noted how society could be similarly seen as a system of individual humans, pulling and pushing against each other. But what held that social system together?

3.3   DAVID HUME

Hume's answer was that society was held together by a moral sentiment. This, however, was not intrinsic to humans, as Hutcheson averred; it was a product of human interaction, and it has evolved over historical time. Hume, then, agreed with Ferguson on this point. However, there may be more than a little Rousseau in his view, for Hume was influenced not only by the English empiricists, but also by thinkers of the French Enlightenment such as Rousseau. In fact, Hume lived in the northwest of France, at La Flèche on the banks of the Loire, during the late 1730s. He read voraciously there and wrote some of his most famous works in France.

Hume on Human Nature

David Hume was born in Edinburgh in 1711. He was bright and entered Edinburgh University when he was about 12 years old. His family pressed him to study law, but he resisted and read philosophy and general learning instead. He read so intensely that he exhausted himself and became physically ill. After a brief and unsuccessful stint at a merchant's office in Bristol, He traveled to France in 1734, to rest.

Rather than resting, Hume continued his reading and writing. He wrote essays on some of the biggest questions in philosophy—on taste, on freedom, on human nature, on the origins of government, on national character, on money, on trade, and many more. He frequented a local monastery to practice the French language and discuss theological questions with the monks. All the while he sought to develop his own philosophical system.

The prime result of his labor was a thick book, *A Treatise of Human Nature*. It has three main parts. Part I, "Of the Understanding," explains how humans acquire knowledge. It describes the origins of ideas, the ideas of space and time, causality, and the reliability of the senses. Part II, "Of the Passions," presents the elaborate mechanisms that constitute human passions or emotions. It argues that passions are the driving forces in human behavior, not reason—that reason plays a subordinate role to passions and emotions. Part III of the book, "Of Morals," discusses justice, virtues, and vices. It does this not in terms of reason, but in terms of beliefs or "feelings." There is, however, no need to postulate an inner "moral sense" behind these feelings, argued Hume. But if morality is the outcome neither of reason nor of an inner moral sense, what is it? How can it be explained if it is neither innate nor a product of reason?

For young Hume, morality was best explained as an outcome of social interaction. His vantage point was presented in the first part of his book, viz., that external sense impressions are the basis of all human knowledge. Our first knowledge of social behavior is, simply, the result of observing the conduct of other people, argued Hume. Conduct which gives us pleasure we consider good; behavior which causes us pain we call bad. As we evolve and mature as humans, we refine these notions. We consider a particular kind of conduct good or bad if it is beneficial or hurtful to the society in which we live.[7] Also, we learn that not only do we observe others and judge their behavior; but others also make judgments about us. And with this realization in mind, we begin to judge our own conduct. This self-assessment, in turn, produces a moral sense in us. Moral sense was, in Hume's view, the outcome of a double dynamic: first, a macro-historical process which involved a long evolution of human society; second, a micro-process through which every member of society is socialized into the norms and values of their particular society.

The first part of the *Treatise* elaborates on Locke's theory of sense, the second part on Hutcheson's Moral Philosophy. The third part argues that human societies evolve through history—and that different societies evolve differently and produce different moral sentiments according to material circumstance. The entire book was inspired by Newton and represents young Hume's effort to develop a philosophical system which could serve as nothing less than a conceptual vantage point for the study of moral philosophy—for ethics, jurisprudence, economics, and politics—in short, for the study of human behavior and society. It was a tall agenda for a man of 25. And although Hume in his later years would brush the effort aside as juvenile, there is no doubt that the views that he developed in La Flèche, consolidated his basic outlook.

The first part of the *Treatise* has, in its various editions, emerged as the most carefully read of Hume's texts. Hume wrote a separate 25-page introduction to the book soon after its publication.[8] Several years later, he rewrote the first part of the *Treatise* and published it as separately as an *Enquiry Concerning Human Understanding* (1748). Here he expanded upon his skeptical theory of knowledge. He argued that the logic of induction could not produce sure and certain knowledge of cause and effect. Also, he claimed that cause could not be observed directly, and that causality could therefore not be inferred directly from observation. What humans refer to as causality is nothing more than the observation of a sequence, of one event following another.[9] "Cause," "force," or "necessary connection" cannot be observed directly. They are all figments of the human imagination. They are ultimately based on habit, Hume concluded.

His skeptical theory of knowledge, with its denial of observable causality and its central concept of habit, had a profound impact on the development of modern philosophy of science.

Essays: Moral, Philosophical, and Literary

Toward the end of his stay in La Flèche, Hume edited 40 of his best essays for publication. A first collection came out in 1741, under the title *Essays:*

Moral, Political, and Literary. If the *Treatise* had fallen still born from the printers' presses, the *Essays* were a critical success.[10] The essays made Hume famous. They were widely read, not only in England and Scotland, but also in America and on the Continent—where numerous translations appeared in German and French. They appeared in 11 editions in Hume's own lifetime. They were reissued in different forms and combinations—sometimes corrected, sometimes with additional commentaries, sometimes abbreviated. Hume worked on these essays continually from 1740 until his death in 1776—by which time he would have edited his 40 original essays many times over; 20 essays would have been added over the years, while 8 were withdrawn.

They covered a vast array of topics. Only some of them addressed political questions, but they tended to spark controversy—as when he argued that the social-contract theories of Thomas Hobbes and John Locke were pure fiction.[11] Many of his essays addressed religious issues. His systematic skepticism often provoked anger—as when Hume denied that humans have an immortal soul, that miracles can be scientifically proven and that there is a life after death.

Hume's essays are steeped in classical learning. They brim with allusions to ancient literature and historical events. Also, they reflect a deep influence from the ancient skeptics.[12] This is particularly evident in those essays which deal with political and theological issues. One of the most conspicuous red threads in Hume's writings is his skepticism about arguments anchored in faith. Indeed, one of his philosophical objectives was to unmask the doctrines and dogmas of belief, be they religious or secular. Consequently, his writings on religion and politics were deeply controversial. His historical writings, by contrast, were much admired, especially his multivolume *History of England*, a series of books on which he worked incessantly during the 1750s. These books were popular and sold so well that they provided Hume with an income that made his life economically secure.

Hume's Moral Philosophy

Hume's writings were deeply influenced by Stoic skepticism and by the tradition of English empiricism—by the visions of John Locke and the celestial mechanics of Isaac Newton. Where Newton collected empirical information by observing the movements of the celestial bodies, Hume obtained knowledge of human society by painstaking investigations of historical events. When he did his research for the *History of England*, he also collected evidence for his philosophy of understanding and his works on moral philosophy.

Hume on Politics and Order. Although Hume followed the methodological empiricism of Newton and Locke, he did not necessarily follow Locke's lead in political philosophy. He rejected, for example, the theory of social contract—the very cornerstone of England's eighteenth-century political philosophy. Hume contested the notion that obedience and government are founded on some original agreement in the past between all members of society. An original act of contract never took place in human history, argued Hume. He brushed the whole notion aside as fiction.

"Of the Original Contract" is one of Hume's most important political essays: First, because his criticism of social-contract theories was so systematic and hard-hitting that it seriously reduced its credence. Second, because he presented an alternative explanation for the advent of states— a development theory that relied on historical evidence. Hume gathered much information about ancient and primitive societies and concluded that they were small and illiterate tribes, unable to formulate even the most basic preconditions of lasting laws; the establishment of a social contract would have been far beyond their comprehension.[13]

If a social contract does not account for the origins of society, what could then account for the authority and obedience that provide social order? What evidence do we have for the advent of the state? Hume had answered these questions already in Part III of his *Treatise of Human Nature*. He relied on historical evidence and developed an argument about historical evolution and the nature of human beings, and the habits, customs, and societies they form—and which, in turn, forms them.

He began by observing distant societies—ancient societies in antiquity and contemporary societies in Asia and America. He concluded that no society consists of individuals; even in the most primitive of societies, human beings organize themselves in families. He began his four-page essay "Of the Origin of Government" by stating that "Man, born in a family, is compelled to maintain society from necessity, from natural inclination and from habit."[14] He then repeated his argument from the *Treatise* and explained that since human beings are so badly adapted to a life in the wild, they are pressed by necessity to develop society.

In phrases that strongly echo Hutcheson, Hume explained that only in society does man have a chance to survive. Also, life in society develops the human skills "and leave[s] him in every respect more satisfied and happy, than 'tis possible for him, in his savage and solitary condition, ever to become."[15] This is so, first because members of a society can bolster their safety and security and protect themselves more efficiently than individual men against enemies, second, because members of a society develop a division of labor which is greatly more productive than if every individual person were to work only for himself, and third, because members of a society care for each other and help each other in case of misfortunes or accidents. Society, Hume concluded, improves the lot of human beings on three accounts: "By the conjunction of forces, our power is augmented. By the partition of employments, our ability increases. And by mutual succour we are less expos'd to fortune and accidents. 'This by this additional force, ability and security, that society becomes advantageous'."[16] This is, in essence, what Hutcheson also had concluded.

Government has evolved through historical time, Hume continued. But why has it evolved? What has driven its evolution? Society is a complex phenomenon and has evolved for many reasons. Two of its most central driving forces, however, are competition and conflict. Hume argues that families evolve into tribes because it helps humans satisfy their basic needs. But tribes enter into competition and conflict with each other and through such conflict evolve institutions of government.

The "first rudiments of government" were established by tribal leaders during military campaigns, argued Hume. Government "arise from quarrels, not among men of the same society, but among those of different societies."[17] From such campaigns evolved both the first institutions of government as well as the first elements of allegiance to governmental authority. Tribal military camps "are the true mothers of cities," Hume concluded.[18] From elementary kinship groups, government progresses through historical stages—from tribes through chieftainships to monarchies. Finally, republics may arise "from the abuses of monarchy and despotic power."[19]

Hume on Money and Trade. Hume's essays on politics criticized established theories of social contract and offered an alternative explanation based on historical evolution. His essays on money and wealth criticized established doctrines of mercantilism—the prevalent economic doctrine of the day. Mercantilism rested on the claim that the earth was finite and that the sum of values in the world was permanent. From this axiom, mercantilists inferred the idea that the volume of international trade was fixed, and that one country could increase its wealth only at the expense of another. They also argued that bullion *was* wealth, and that the government must play an important role in the economy by making sure that the country accumulated bullion—by seizing the wealth of others if necessary.

Hume ridiculed these arguments. First, he denied the claim that bullion was the same as wealth; the mercantilists confused the wheels of trade with the oil which renders their motion smooth and easy.[20] Wealth, he argued, was not a thing but a process—or more precisely, a process of labor. This idea made Hume deny, second, that the values in the world were an expression of the finite resources of the earth. Value was, rather, created as labor transformed the resources of the earth into commodities. As to war, Hume argued that although war could extort land and resources from others, it would also entail two intrinsic costs: it would destroy trade and convert productive laborers into unproductive—if not destructive—soldiers. If a country could employ its young men as productive laborers (instead of soldiers), it would not only increase its own wealth, it would increase the wealth of other countries as well: for the increased wealth would enable that country to buy more goods from other countries, whose production would, in turn, be stimulated to satisfy this demand and whose exports would grow as a result.

Some of Hume's essays refuted mercantilist claims and developed different sides of his own argument. In his essay "Of Money" Hume elaborated on his labor-centered theory of value by claiming that trade, wealth, and industry "are in reality nothing but a stock of labor."[21] In "On Commerce" he agreed with the mercantilists that when the government printed new money, money would cause prices to rise. However, he disagreed with them when he added that prices would rise only if the volume of goods remained fixed. If an increase in money supply could also provide temporary stimuli in both production and employment, and if this, in turn, increased the output of goods, then prices might not rise. In fact, a government might well increase the money supply if this stimulated employment, because this would mobilize more labor which would, in turn, create more wealth.

Hume contributed greatly to the economic debate of his day. He criticized the prevalent mercantilist doctrines on which English trade was based. But he also contributed to the formulation of a new, labor-centered theory of value and to a new, free-market-based economic theory. Hume's economic arguments undoubtedly influenced his younger friend, Adam Smith. How great this influence was, is still a matter of deep controversy.

3.4 ADAM SMITH

Adam Smith was born in the Scottish fishing village of Kirkaldy in 1723. At the age of 14 he entered the University of Glasgow. In 1738 and -39 he followed the lectures of Francis Hutcheson in Moral Philosophy—as Hume had done a decade earlier. In 1740 Smith won a scholarship to Oxford. It was a huge disappointment. After the brilliant lectures and the active guidance of Hutcheson, he found his Oxford teachers idle and incompetent by comparison. However, the university had a first-rate library, and Smith spent his Oxford years there, deeply immersed in self-study. One of the few instances in which the university involved itself in his education, Smith recalled later, was when a faculty member in 1740 interrupted his reading, warned him that the author he was reading was an atheist and his texts subversive of morality. The professor promptly confiscated Smith's copy—of David Hume's brand-new *Treatise on Human Nature*.

Smith knew and admired Hume long before the two of them met. When they met, around 1750 in Glasgow, Smith was 26, Hume was 38. Smith had moved to Glasgow to teach Moral Philosophy—taking over the chair that Francis Hutcheson had occupied when Hume and Smith were students in the city.

Smith's Works on Moral Philosophy

Smith chose to follow the example of his old teacher and present comprehensive lectures in morals, jurisprudence, politics, and economics along Hutcheson's lines. From his lectures on morals and jurisprudence, Smith developed his first book, *The Theory of Moral Sentiments* (1759). It argued that moral sentiments and values are not natural (as Hutcheson had argued), but that they are results of social interaction and that they develop through history. He agreed, then, with the historical argument of Hume, who had claimed that societies evolved over time and that, as humans cooperated for survival and reproduction, a moral sense was instilled in humans by habit.

From his lectures on politics and economics Smith developed his second book, *The Wealth of Nations* (1776). What is it that makes some nations rich whereas others remain poor, Smith asked on its opening pages? And he immediately gave his famous answer: labor and the division of labor in society.

The Wealth of Nations. What makes nations rich? This is one of the classic questions in Political Economy. And Smith formulated one of the most authoritative answers in the field. The *Wealth of Nations* has stirred political passions for over two centuries. Even in the twenty-first century, debates about it sometimes deteriorate into shouting matches.

The book is divided into five parts. The first part contains the most famous arguments and is well worth a closer look. The first chapter of the first part is entitled "Of the Division of Labor" and introduces Smith's famous example of a pin factory. If one solitary man were to make pins, Smith writes, he could hardly, even "with his utmost industry, make one pin a day, and certainly could not make twenty."[22] But if several men cooperated and divided the work between them, they could easily multiply the pin production:

> One man draws out the wire, another straights it, a third cuts it, a fourth points it, a fifth grinds it at the top for receiving the head; to make the head requires two or three distinct operations; to put it on, is a peculiar business, to whiten the pins is another; it is even a trade by itself to put them into the paper...[23]

The business of making a pin, then, can be divided between ten or eleven different operations. If labor is so finely divided that each operation is given to one man, a team of ten can make several pounds of pins a day, argued Smith. Since each pound contains "upwards of four thousand pounds of a middling size ... ten persons, therefore could make among them upwards of forty-eight thousand pins in a day."[24] Such an enormous increase in productivity—from one pin for a solitary man to nearly 50,000 for a team of ten—can take place when individual workers specialize.

In a society where labor is specialized, each man can produce a great quantity of special goods and can then exchange some of them for other goods produced by other specialized men. However, this is possible only when each man has the opportunity to exchange his own goods for those of other men. Thus, *exchange* is a necessary precondition for a social division of labor which, in turn, increases the efficiency of production and creates wealth in society. Exchange takes place in a market. And the division of labor "must always be limited by the extent of the market," Smith concluded.[25]

In the early stages of history, exchange involved barter—when humans were hunters or shepherds, they might barter nuts for berries or fish for meat. However, as the market expanded, barter was replaced by more regular trade. At that point, human interaction evolved from the primitive stage of hunting through agriculture and on toward the commercial stage of history. Towns were established along the way. Money was invented. Investments were made to satisfy demands for specific goods.

Urbanization, commercial shipping, and the building of canals and roads are great stimuli for market growth and for the social division of labor, argues Smith. Money and finance make trade and investments much easier. It contributes to the growth of wealth and the evolution of social complexity.

In primitive society a good may be made by a man who then brings it to the market for barter or sale. In modern society the process is more complex. Agents emerge between the producer and the seller. Over time, those agents interconnect to institute long chains of interaction and trans- action. Smith used the example of an ordinary wool coat to drive the point home. In modern society a coat is the product of the joint labor of a great multitude of specialized agents.

The modern market, in other words, is a complicated web of interac- tion; it involves innumerable interdependent actors and is often world- wide in scope.

The Legacy and Originality of Adam Smith. Smith was not the first person to ask what made some nations rich whereas others remained poor. Neither was he the first person to propose the answer that labor was the source of all value and that a social division of labor was a source of productivity and wealth. Nor was Smith the first person to argue that society evolved from primitive society through successive states to its modern form. The basic components that went into Smith's argu- ment, then, were not original. Yet, when Smith put them all together, he produced a masterpiece. Even his critics recognized the importance of his *Wealth of Nations.*

One reason for this is that these components are more extensively applied and the argument more fully developed than in previous works. Smith spent over 20 years to write the book, and he honed his terms finely and used them with great precision. Also, he illustrated his argu- ments with clever examples—the pin factory and the commodity chains involved in the making of a woolen coat are examples of great didactical value. Smith also applied his argument convincingly, backing it up with historical cases as well as contemporary applications that demonstrated their explanatory power.

Another reason why *The Wealth of Nations* is hailed as a great classic is that it presented an impressive philosophical system of political economy. The comprehensive scope of this system may be the most impressive feature of *The Wealth of Nations*. Smith, in short, illustrated well an important point argued by his good friend, David Hume, that the whole is more than the sum of the parts.

3.5   CONCLUSIONS

The authors of the Scottish Enlightenment had all studied Newton's work. They admired it deeply and sought to emulate its logical structure and import this into their own philosophical systems. Newton had shown that, in the sky, there is a sort of natural, harmonious system generated by the properties of the different celestial objects and held together by the force of gravity. Hutcheson, Hume, and Smith considered that, on earth, the interaction of human beings are similarly balanced and contribute to order and a natural harmony. This consideration is visible in David Hume's discussions of political order—perhaps most clearly in his discussions of order among states. In his essay "Of the Balance of Trade," he shows how wealth and order in Europe are sustained by economic transactions and trade. In "Of the Balance of Power," he shows how the behavior of each European state is restricted by an overall system of power.[26]

The influence of Newton is even more apparent in the writings of Adam Smith. He saw Newton as a great genius who developed a simple and elegant system out of apparent chaos.[27] Like Newton, Smith first directed his scientific gaze toward the sky and wrote a "History of Astronomy." Later, Smith turned his attention toward social affairs and wrote books on Moral Philosophy. He turned to history to collect his data, but he retained Newton's scientific lead by applying his analytic skills to human affairs. *The Theory of Moral Sentiments* and *The Wealth of Nations* have the same notion of "system" that informs Smith's essay on astronomy. Smith invokes "the invisible hand" in all three books to denote a force that keeps individual actors in their proper systemic orbit—whether these actors are planets or people and their system celestial or social.[28]

The Enlightenment ideas of Reason, Rights, and Progress are apparent in the writings of Hutcheson, Hume, and Smith, but in varying degrees.

They all agreed that humans are equipped with Reason. But they also agreed that humans are not driven by reason alone. They acknowledged that passion also played a role in human life. And they emphasized what they called "moral sentiments" as an important driving force in human behavior. They argued that humans are equipped with a rich variety of such sentiments—selfishness, faith, love, hate, anger, envy, and others. In this emphasis on sentiments, the Scottish thinkers indicated a budding critique of Enlightenment orthodoxy, signaling an early reaction to its rationalist optimism.

The influence of the Scottish Enlightenment views reached far beyond Scotland and the British Isles. Scottish ideas and attitudes were held in high esteem in the rest of Europe and were considered an integral part of the Enlightenment revolution. They were also carried across the Atlantic as part of a growing Scottish diaspora in the Americas, where they affected philosophical and scientific development in the United States and Canada.

America's Founding Fathers read Hutcheson, Smith, Hume, and other contributors to the Scottish Enlightenment. They were affected by their views.[29] Hutcheson's ideas influenced Thomas Jefferson and their optimistic echoes may be traced in the preamble of *The Declaration of Independence*.[30] This *Declaration* differs in tone from *The American Constitution*, which is marked by the more measured views of James Madison. He was more in tune with the skeptical anthropology of David Hume.[31]

NOTES

1. Francis Hutcheson, *A Short Introduction to Moral Philosophy, in Three Books* (Glasgow: R. & A. Foulis, 1753), pp. 68ff.
2. Hume's essay "Of the immortality of the Soul", in particular, ruffled many feathers. Hume chose to leave it out of his later essay collections. It was too radical for its time. More radical still was his *Dialogue Concerning Natural Religion*. His friends read it and convinced him to withhold it from publication, reminding him that Thomas Aikenhead, an eighteen-year-old student at Edinburg, had been executed for the crime of blasphemy in 1697.
3. The term was coined by William Scott in his Hutcheson biography: *Francis Hutcheson: His Life, Teaching and Position in the History of Philosophy* (Cambridge: Cambridge University Press, 1900).

4. A spirit of pragmatic progress, expressed in the "improving move-
ment", were applied to all aspects of life. It was manifested in the
engineering feats of James Watt, in the medical doctors William
Cullen and William and John Hunter, in John Sinclair and John
Playfair of statistical fame, in William Smellie, the founder of the
Encyclopaedia Britannica, and in the works of John Millar and
Joseph Black.

5. Hutcheson defined Moral Philosophy as "the art of regulating
the whole of life" and divided it into Ethics and Virtue on
the one hand and Jurisprudence on the other. He then divided
jurisprudence into three subjects: What he called Private rights and
Natural liberty; Familial rights (which we today might recognize
as Economics); and, finally, State and Individual Rights (which we
would later provide the basic arguments of Political Science). See
Hutcheson, *A Short Introduction to Moral Philosophy*; also Francis
Hutcheson, *A System of Moral Philosophy*, Vol. 1 (Glasgow: R. &
A. Foulis, 1755 [1747]).

6. Hutcheson *A System of Moral Philosophy*, Vol. 1, pp. 288ff.

7. David Hume, *A Treatise of Human Nature* (Oxford: Clarendon
Press, 1978 [1740]), pp. 978, 470.

8. The *Treatise of Human Nature* had an ambitious intention. When
it was published it received a disappointing reception. Hume's
immediate reaction was that the work was not properly understood.
So he quickly wrote an explanation—a 25 page pamphlet entitled
An Abstract of a Book lately Published (1740).

9. Hume argued that people may observe how some things always
appear together—e.g., when a rolling billiard ball (A) hits a
stationary billiard ball (B), the first ball stops and the second starts
rolling. People then make the inference that the two things are
somehow causally connected—that A caused B to roll. However, all
they have observed is a succession of events—and such successions
and co-relations are all that observation will ever give us, argued
Hume.

10. Hume prepared a second volume of essays which was published the
following year (as volume two under the same title). Seven years
later, Hume published three longer essays in a small volume entitled *Three Essays: Moral and Political*. In 1752 Hume issues a large
number of new essays under the title *Political Discourses*. These
four basic volumes of essays, together with one or two chapters in

Part III of his *Treatise of Human Nature*, constitute the scattered core of Hume's writings of political philosophy.

11. David Hume, "Of the Original Contract", in *Essays: Moral, Political, and Literary* (Indianapolis: Liberty Classics, 1985), pp. 464–487.

12. As is also apparent in one of his longest essays (see David Hume, "The Skeptic", in *Essays: Moral, Political, and Literary*, pp. 159–181.

13. See Hume, "Of the Original Contract", *passim*.

14. David Hume, "Of the Origin of Government", in *Essays: Moral, Political, and Literary* [Note 15], p. 37.

15. Hume, *A Treatise* [Note 10], p. 485.

16. *Idem.*

17. Hume, *A Treatise* [Note 10], pp. 539ff.

18. *Ibid.*, p. 541.

19. *Ibid.*, p. 540.

20. David Hume, "On Money", in *Essays: Moral, Political, and Literary* [Note 14], p. 281.

21. *Ibid.*, p. 268.

22. Adam Smith, *The Wealth of Nations* (New York: Modern Library 1965 [1776]), p. 4.

23. *Ibid.*

24. *Ibid.*, p. 5.

25. *Ibid.*, p. 17.

26. David Hume, "Of the Balance of Power", in *Essays: Moral, Political, and Literary* [Note 15], pp. 332–342.

27. Adam Smith, The History of Astronomy", in *Essays on Philosophical Subjects*, ed. W.P.D. Wightman and J.C. Bryce, Vol. III of the Glasgow Edition of the Works and Correspondence of Adam Smith (Indianapolis: Liberty Fund, 1982), pp. 33–106 at p. 104.

28. Smith, *Wealth of Nations*, p. 423; Adam Smith, *The Theory of Moral Sentiment* (Indianapolis: Liberty Classics, 1982 [1759]), p. 184; and Smith, "History of Astronomy", Part VI, p. 2.

29. Daniel W. Howe, "Why the Scottish Enlightenment Was Useful to the framers of the American Constitution", in *Comparative Studies in Society and History*, Vol. 31, No. 3 (1989), pp. 572–587; Arthur Herman, *How the Scots Invented the Modern World* (New York: Crown Publishing Group, 2001); and James Buchan,

Crowded with Genius: Edinburgh's Moment of the Mind (New York: HarperCollins, 2003).

30. Garry Wills, *Inventing America: Jefferson's Declaration of Independence* (New York: Doubleday, 1978).

31. Mark G. Spencer, "Hume and Madison on Faction", in *David Hume and Eighteenth-Century America* (Rochester: University of Rochester Press, 2005; reissued by Boydell & Brewer, 2012), pp. 154–187.

FURTHER READINGS

Aiken, Henry David. "An Interpretation of Hume's Theory of the Place of Reason in Ethics and Politics", in *Ethics*, Vol. 90, No. 1 (October 1979).

Baier, Annette C. "Moralism and Cruelty: Reflections on Hume and Kant", in *Ethics*, Vol. 103, No. 3 (April 1993).

Griswold, Charles L., Jr. "Religion and Community: Adam Smith on the Virtue of Liberty", in *Theoria: A Journal of Social and Political Theory*, No. 102 (December 2003).

Jones, Harold B. "Marcus Aurelius, the Stoic Ethic, and Adam Smith", in *Journal of Business Ethics*, Vol. 95, No. 1 (August 2010).

McRorie, Christina. "Adam Smith, Ethicist: A Case for Reading Political Economy as Moral Anthropology", in *The Journal of Religious Ethics*, Vol. 43, No. 4 (December 2015).

Norman, Jesse. *Adam Smith: What He Thought and Why it Matters* (Penguin, 2019)

Rasmussen, Dennis C. *The Infidel and the Professor: David Hume, Adam Smith, and the Friendship that Shaped Modern Thought* (Princeton University Press, 2017).

Sabl, Andrew. "The Last Artificial Virtue: Hume on Toleration and Its Lessons", in *Political Theory*, Vol. 37, No. 4 (August 2009).

Sagar, Paul. "Smith and Rousseau, after Hume and Mandeville", in *Political Theory*, Vol. 46, No. 1 (February 2018).

Samuels, Warren J. "The Political Economy of Adam Smith", in *Ethics*, Vol. 87, No. 3 (April 1977).

Scott, William. *Francis Hutcheson: His Life, Teaching and Position in the History of Philosophy* (Cambridge University Press, 1900).

Shapiro, Michael J. "Eighteenth Century Intimations of Modernity: Adam Smith and the Marquis de Sade", in *Political Theory*, Vol. 21, No. 2 (May 1993).

CHAPTER 4

The American Enlightenment: Thomas Paine, Thomas Jefferson, and James Madison

Sabrina P. Ramet

Abstract America's leading Enlightenment thinkers, Thomas Paine, Thomas Jefferson, and James Madison were key figures in bringing about the American Revolution and the birth of the American Republic. In the course of so doing, they defended the principles of individual liberty, human equality, and religious tolerance. Grounded in the Enlightenment tradition, they subscribed to the doctrine of Natural Law, and also believed that people have certain inalienable, natural rights. While all three of them defended religious freedom and religious tolerance—alongside freedoms of speech, press, and assembly—Paine nonetheless criticized Christianity relentlessly in a work in which he subjected the Bible to mockery, founding his critique on an appeal to reason.

Keywords Individual liberty · Equality · Religious tolerance · Natural law · Inalienable rights · Freedom of assembly · Freedom of the press · Deism · Federalism

The leading figures in the American Enlightenment were heavily influenced by British and French writers, especially Locke and, where Jefferson and Madison were concerned, also Montesquieu. Five themes emerged in their writings and activity: Liberalism, Republicanism, Deism, Toleration, and Scientific Progress.[1] Under *liberalism* was understood that people were born with innate (or natural) rights and therefore that the authority of government was, or had to be, based on the consent of the governed. *Republicanism* is closely related to this, entailing that government officials should be elected by the country's citizens for fixed terms of office. *Deism* (see also Box 4.3) emerged as a product of religious skepticism and held that religious belief should be based on reason and that God should not be expected to be actively involved in human affairs. *Toleration*, especially religious toleration, was embraced by Jefferson, Madison, and other American Enlightenment thinkers as both a recognition of people's liberty and innate rights, and the effective remedy to avoid a recurrence of the interreligious warfare which Europe had endured in the sixteenth and seventeenth centuries (especially in the French Wars of Religion, 1562–98, and the Thirty Years' War, 1618–48). And finally, as Shane Ralston notes, "Enlightenment enthusiasm for *scientific discovery* was directedly related to the growth of deism and skepticism about received religious doctrine."[2]

The most prominent American Enlightenment thinkers/activists (in alphabetical order) were: John Adams (1735–1826), Benjamin Franklin (1706–1790), Thomas Jefferson (1743–1826), James Madison (1751–1836), and Thomas Paine (1737–1809). This chapter focuses on the lives, writings, and activities of Jefferson, Madison, and Paine.

4.1   POLITICAL ENGAGEMENT

Without Paine, Jefferson, and Madison, history might have taken an entirely different course. Paine's contribution with his writing to the American Revolution was crucial, as General (later President) George Washington recognized. Jefferson drafted the Declaration of Independence and, as third president, repealed the notorious Alien and Sedition Acts passed by his predecessor John Adams (see Box 4.1), which severely restricted freedom of speech. Madison collaborated with Alexander Hamilton (see Box 4.2) and John Jay in writing a series of papers later collected under the title *The Federalist* (or sometimes, *The Federalist Papers*), making the argument that the weak confederation under which the newly independent American states were attempting to operate was dysfunctional, and thereby persuaded the states to agree to a tighter union. Madison was also crucial in pushing through the Bill of Rights, and later served as fourth president of the United States. The body of writings which they left behind not only played a critical role in framing the arguments of their day but continue to have an influence even today, as may be seen in the continued frequency of citations to their insights. Jefferson and Madison had read the works of Locke and Sidney, among others and endeavored to create a constitutional-political framework embodying the principles they had found in the writings of the English Enlightenment.

Box 4.1: John Adams

John Adams (1735–1826), second President of the United States, was born in Braintree (now Quincy), Massachusetts. He studied law at Harvard University, served in the Continental Congress 1774–1777, and joined George Washington's government as vice president, later occupying the presidency from 1797 to 1801. Adams had read Plato and Thucydides in the original Greek, Tacitus in the original Latin, and also the works of John Locke, David Hume, Francis Hutcheson, and Henry St. John Bolingbroke. In his treatise, *Thoughts on Government* (1776), he wrote that the purpose of government was to assure "the greatest quantity of human happiness." As author of the three-volume *Defence of the Constitutions of Government of the United States of America*, published in 1787, he warned against efforts to make a fundamental break with the past as well as efforts to transform human nature, both of which he considered utopian and dangerous. As president, he signed the Naturalization Act (later repealed), which raised the residency requirement for gaining citizenship from five to 14 years; he also signed the Sedition Act (also later repealed), which made it a crime to publish "false, scandalous and malicious" writings against the president and the Congress; the Congress was, at the time, controlled by the Federalist Party, of which Adams was a leading member.

Box 4.2: Alexander Hamilton

Alexander Hamilton (1755/57–1804), America's first Secretary of the Treasury, was born on the Island of Nevis in the West Indies. Educated at King's College (later renamed Columbia University), he served as an officer in the Continental Army, was elected to the State Assembly of New York, and contributed 51 of the 85 essays which comprised *The Federalist* (later also called *The Federalist Papers*), arguing for the adoption of the proposed constitution. Hamilton thought that political parties would promote disorder and instability but, as the Federalist Party came into being, Hamilton assumed the leadership of the party, because the party supported his policies. Hamilton was extremely well read and had read the works of Grotius, Pufendorf, Locke, Montesquieu, and Hume, among others, accepting the Natural Law theories advocated by Grotius, Pufendorf, and Locke. Thus, in arguing as a lawyer in the case of Rutgers v. Waddington, he urged that governments were bound by Natural Law. He viewed religion and morality as the most important buttresses of "political prosperity" and depicted corruption as the greatest threat to democratic life.

When one considers the thinking of Thomas Paine,[3] Thomas Jefferson, and James Madison, one may well be struck by the general agreement among them. Whether one considers their views on government or religious liberty or slavery or the indigenous nations of the continent that Europeans called "the New World," one finds a general harmony of values and perspectives. There may be incidental differences between Jefferson and Madison, but the two men, together with Paine—like Sidney and Locke, radicals in their time—all hoped to build an American Republic founded on the principles of individual rights, equality, and religious tolerance. Like Locke, Jefferson and Madison wanted to guarantee civic freedom only to male citizens with property. These principles were to be applied in equal measure to all male citizens—the question, then, was how to define citizenship and, on this point, Paine would part from Jefferson and Madison (a point to which we shall return in due course in the section on the indigenous nations).

The three men were close contemporaries, Paine having been born in 1737, Jefferson in 1743, and Madison in 1751, and Jefferson was friends with both Paine and Madison.[4] Madison was the most bookish of the three, while Paine achieved success in his lifetime, not only with his writings, but also with his design for an iron bridge[5]; Jefferson's interests included botany, crop cycles, and whaling; he also produced more than 500 architectural designs of which the earliest were sketches for the construction of Monticello (his house), and perfected a design for a moldboard plough which would be recognized with the award of a gold medal from a French agricultural society (the Societé d'agriculture du department de la Seine).[6]

Today, Thomas Paine is remembered for his *Common Sense*, which scholars credit with inspiring the American Revolution,[7] and for his *Rights of Man*, Parts 1 and 2, which electrified France and Britain, putting him on William Pitt's "most wanted" list. Paine also served as aide-de-camp to General Nathanael Greene in General Washington's army, was elected to the French National Assembly, drafted a Declaration of Rights for France (possibly in collaboration with Antoine-Nicolas de Condorcet),[8] and, at the instigation of Jefferson, Madison, and President Washington's Attorney General, Edmund Randolph, was even offered a position in Washington's cabinet, as Postmaster General.[9]

Jefferson and Madison both served in the Virginia legislature, subsequently serving as secretary of state (in Jefferson's case, to George Washington; in Madison's case, to Jefferson), before serving eight years each as president. Jefferson, who served as vice president to President John Adams (1797–1801) before succeeding him as president, as well as president of the American Philosophical Society, drafted the U.S. Declaration of Independence in which, in his original draft, he included a long section denouncing the slave trade, while Madison's role both as the chief writer of the constitution and in drafting and pushing forward the Bill of Rights stands as a notable achievement.[10]

John Locke was one of the most important influences on both Jefferson and Madison. Among other things, Jefferson's "Bill for Establishing Religious Freedom," presented to the House of Delegates in Virginia in 1779, contained paraphrases of several passages from Locke's *Letter Concerning Toleration*,[11] while the opening passages of the Declaration of Independence (1776), establishing a right to revolution in the face of injustice, clearly reflect the influence of Locke and Algernon Sidney, and Locke would later describe Sidney's *Discourses Concerning Government* as "a rich treasure of republican principles, supported by copious and cogent arguments, and adorned with the finest flowers of science[,]...probably the best elementary book of the principles of government, as founded in natural right, which has ever been published in any language."[12] (Jefferson was apparently equally enthusiastic about Antoine Louis Claude Destutt de Tracy's *Commentary and Review of Montesquieu*, which he praised, on one occasion, as "the soundest text in government ever written."[13]) For his part, Madison was influenced by Locke's *Essay Concerning Human Understanding*, perhaps especially by the British philosopher's discussion, in that work, of the divergent motivations which drive people to pursue different ends.

Jefferson and Madison had also read the works of ancient Greek and Roman writers (including Cicero), and Montesquieu.[14] Jefferson was also influenced by the writings of Lord Bolingbroke, Francis Bacon, Sir James Stewart, Lord Kames, Baron d'Holbach, and Francis Hutcheson,[15] while, for Madison, David Hume's writings were a crucial source for his thinking about faction and representation.[16] In addition, Madison was clearly influenced by his reading of Aristotle.[17]

4.2   DEMOCRACY AND THE PURPOSE OF GOVERNMENT

All three men situated their understanding of the purposes of government and the practical way in which to organize government within the context of the theory of Universal Reason (the moral law) and their belief that people enjoyed "God-given" rights. All three were cautiously hopeful that the good in people would triumph over the evil, within the context of the democratic project, although all of them, but most obviously Madison, saw the need for safeguards to be taken. Jefferson, to be sure, held that "[m]an was destined for society. His morality, therefore, was to be formed to this object. He was endowed with a sense of right and wrong, merely relative to this. This sense is as much a part of his nature, as the sense of hearing, seeing, feeling."[18]

Madison, by contrast, while not denying that humankind might be improved by good education and other factors, perhaps paid greater attention to humanity's shortcomings. And hence, in *Federalist* no. 55, we find him striking a balance:

> As there is a degree of depravity in mankind which requires a certain degree of circumspection and distrust, so there are other qualities in human nature which justify a certain portion of esteem and confidence. Republican government presupposes the existence of these qualities in a higher degree than another other form [of government].[19]

But, for Madison, the depravity which one encountered in people was sufficient to warrant the establishment of institutional and legal safeguards. Madison wrote further, in a famous passage:

> If men were angels, no government would be necessary. If angels were to govern men, neither external nor internal controls on government would be necessary. In framing a government which is to be administered by men

over men, [however,] the great difficulty lies in this: you must first enable the government to control the governed; and in the next place oblige it to control itself.[20]

Thomas Paine had already anticipated this line of thinking in *Common Sense*, in suggesting that "government...[was] rendered necessary by the inability of moral virtue to govern the world."[21]

For Paine, thus, government was "a necessary evil" which had the assurance of *security* as its chief end.[22] In order to achieve that, government should be characterized by rule by fixed, known laws, rather than by the rule of one person or group of persons,[23] and he urged that "the law ought to prohibit only actions hurtful to society."[24] When Edmund Burke, the Irish-born member of the British parliament, published his *Reflections on the Revolution in France* in 1790, Paine was infuriated. Denouncing the French Revolution, which was still in its early phase, for disregarding tradition, Burke had maintained that

...the accumulated wisdom of the past...was a far better guide to political behavior than abstract 'prattling about the rights of men,' which had the dangerous tendency to overthrow long-established institutions and to upset the 'principles of natural subordination' which stable government required.[25]

Paine considered this contention absurd, and, in his *Rights of Man, Part 1*, published a year later, denied that any generation could bind posterity for all time to come. Jefferson concurred with Paine that there was no reason for people to feel bound by the political decisions taken by their ancestors,[26] urging, on the contrary, in a letter to James Madison, that "the earth should belong always to the living generation."[27]

Jefferson spelled out his vision for good government in his inaugural address in 1801, urging respect for the "sacred principle, that[,] though the will of the majority is in all cases to prevail, that will, to be rightful, must be reasonable; [and] that the minority possess their equal rights, which equal laws must protect, and to violate which would be oppression."[28] He continued by enumerating what he considered "the essential principles" of good government, and included here civil supremacy over the military, trials by impartial jury, the encouragement of agriculture and commerce, and freedoms of religion, press, and person (under *habeas corpus*).[29] He had previously argued, on another occasion, for the separation of executive, legislative, and judicial powers as a vital element in any government that wishes to call itself democratic.[30]

Madison was of the same mind and, soon thereafter, warned, in *Federalist* No. 47, of the danger of uniting legislative and executive powers in one person or "body of magistrates."[31] Madison's starting point, in *Federalist No. 14*, was to distinguish *republican government* (today, we would say *representative government*) from *democracy*. Democracy, in his account, consisted in citizens meeting and taking decisions collectively; such a system could work only within a small area, such as a small town, and would, in any event, be an unstable and dangerous system. A republic, on the contrary, might be established and sustained over a much larger area.[32]

The challenge posed by conflicts between and among organized interests—which Madison, following Hume, called *factions*—was very much on his mind. Hume had warned that "Factions subvert government, render laws impotent, and beget the fiercest animosities among men of the same nation, who ought to give mutual assistance and protection to each other."[33] Madison, like Hume, saw some tendencies toward antisocial behavior on the part of people, tendencies which he, again like Hume, believed were only aggravated by faction. Now, in his famous No. 10, Madison addressed this challenge. Here he defined a *faction* as "a number of citizens, whether amounting to a majority or minority of the whole, who are united and actuated by some common impulse of passion, or of interest, adverse to the rights of other citizens, or to the permanent and aggregate interests of the community."[34] Proceeding on the basis of this definition, he found that "[t]he latent causes of faction are...sown in the nature of man," whether one thinks of differences of religious belief or different ideas about government or other matters.[35] To cure "the mischiefs" of faction, he rejected undertakings to socialize people to the extent that they all would have the same opinions and interests, or to simply destroy people's freedom. He also dismissed as "vain" the hope that the nation might always be guided by enlightened statesmen. That left a fourth alternative, viz., to construct the system in such a way that there would be checks on the ability of factions, whether within the government or in the society, to tyrannize over others or of ambitious politicians seeking to overthrow the constitutional order. Madison argued that the larger the republic, the greater the number of interests and contending parties, and thus the greater possibility for them to act as checks on each other.[36]

As for the revolution which set the thirteen colonies on the road to independence and union, this was justified by Paine on the grounds that monarchy was contrary to human reason, by Jefferson on the grounds that "whenever any form of government becomes destructive of these ends [the assurance of life, liberty and the pursuit of happiness], it is the right of the people to alter or to abolish it, and to institute a new government,"[37] and by Madison, quoting from the Declaration of Independence, by reference to "the transcendent and precious right of the people to 'abolish or alter their governments as to them shall seem most likely to effect their safety and happiness.'".[38]

Finally, as to the purpose of government, where Paine had connected it to security and Jefferson had linked it to the assurance of people's rights to "life, liberty, and the pursuit of happiness," Madison declared simply that "*Justice* is the end of government."[39]

4.3   The Indigenous Nations

Security, justice, liberty, the pursuit of happiness, and even life itself were guaranteed to citizens as well as to legal immigrants (legal under U.S. law), but not to people deemed to be living in "the state of nature," while slaves were guaranteed security and justice only, and even those were guaranteed not by the government but by the slaves' owners, according to their interpretations of these concepts. The indigenous peoples of North America, in the eighteenth and nineteenth centuries included, *among others*, Iroquois, Chickasaws, Cherokees, Choctaws, Seminoles, and Creeks, but were commonly called Indians by white immigrants (some of whom referred to themselves as "Native Americans" and formed the xenophobic Know Nothing Party in 1844[40]). The indigenous nations were judged to be in a state of nature which—for the colonists—meant without "real" property rights and even, for some, without the right to life. These nations have been assigned various names by Europeans, European immigrants, and others, names such as Indians (based on a misconception), Native Americans (a racist term), and Amerindians (attempting to fuse two misunderstandings together). Thus, we find that "Massachusetts colony was at the time [prior to the Revolution] offering a hundred pounds for Indian scalps taken from males over the age of twelve, while female scalps brought fifty pounds."[41] The slaughter of the indigenous peoples would continue for another century, with many survivors fleeing to Canada after the Great Sioux War of 1876–1877.

But this was a betrayal of the Enlightenment. None of the three figures considered here advocated genocide. On the contrary, they all supported the rights of indigenous people to life, liberty, and the pursuit of happiness—albeit with some important differences between Paine and the other two figures. Paine, for his part, championed the rights of the indigenous nations to their land and to their way of life.[42] Jefferson was also sympathetic to the indigenous population, devoting a chapter in his *Notes on Virginia* to describing those indigenous cultures with which he had some acquaintance and setting aside a room at Monticello for a collection of artifacts of indigenous nations. Going against the general thinking of his time, he proposed that a law be passed making the penalty for killing an indigenous person the same as for killing an immigrant from Europe or his or her descendants.[43] But, for Jefferson, indigenous rights to enjoy the fruits of citizenship were contingent upon their assimilating into "white" American society. To this end, Jefferson cast "white" Americans in the role of teachers, who would introduce the indigenous people to European/"white" American implements and practices of animal husbandry, agriculture, household arts, and so forth.[44]

Members of indigenous nations were not enthusiastic about being submerged into white culture, however, and, in his second inaugural address in 1805, Jefferson bemoaned the fact that "...the endeavors to enlighten them on the fate which awaits their present course of life, to induce them to exercise their reason, follow its dictates, and change their pursuits with the change of circumstances, have powerful obstacles to encounter."[45] Jefferson came to believe that the indigenous peoples could be (almost) equal to people of European stock and, in 1808, he suggested that intermarriage between indigenous people and immigrants from Europe and their descendants might promote both integration and assimilation.[46] On the other hand, for those indigenous people who refused to assimilate, Jefferson showed little compassion. Already at the dawn of his second term, having doubled the size of the country through the Louisiana Purchase (in which payment was made to France, not to the indigenous nations that lived there), Jefferson mused that the time would come when English-speaking immigrants and their descendants would "cover the whole northern, if not the southern continent, with a people speaking the same language, governed in similar forms, and by similar laws."[47] As early as 1784, scarcely a year after the American Revolutionary War came to an end, Jefferson sketched a map which would be reflected in the Land Ordinance of that year. The map anticipated that indigenous homelands in the "Northwest Territory" (the region which today comprises Michigan, Illinois, Indiana, and Ohio) would be incorporated into the United States. To support this expansionist project, Jefferson favored altering the demographic balance in the region by promoting the colonization of the region by immigrants from Europe or their descendants. Washington, Jefferson, and members of the Congress told themselves that the Northwest Territory was "unsettled wilderness," whereas it was the homeland of the Confederacy of Indigenous Nations.[48] Madison's thinking closely paralleled Jefferson's. Already in *Federalist* No. 42, Madison mused that "[w]hat description of Indians are to be deemed members of a State is not yet settled,"[49] and, as he explained in a letter to James Monroe in 1784, "[b]y Indian[s] not members of a State, must be meant those...who do not live within the body of the Society, or whose Persons or property form no objects of its laws."[50] In other words, indigenous people classified as "not members of a State" were considered to be in a state of nature and, by that virtue, to enjoy no legal protection of their property or even of their lives. In a subsequent letter to Monroe, however, he wrote that Congress had made provision to punish crimes against indigenous people.[51]

In his inaugural address (1809), Madison echoed Jefferson in declaring his administration's commitment, as he saw it, "to lift the American aborigines from degradation and wretchedness into a civilized state."[52] Three years later, by which time the United States was at war with Britain, President Madison entertained 29 local chiefs at the White House, and urged them to settle their differences with each other and to devote themselves to cattle- and sheep-breeding, agriculture, and weaving,[53] in other words to begin to assimilate into white culture. Yet it should be stressed that Madison, like Jefferson, recognized that the locals, like all persons whether "members of a State" or not, enjoyed natural rights. And, in recognition thereof, when in 1815 "white" settlers encroached upon some lands belonging to indigenous people and attempted to seize them for themselves, Madison sent soldiers to drive away the settlers. Later, in response to a deputation of Cherokees (on behalf of themselves and another tribe), Madison sent word to Commissioner Andrew Jackson that "The President is determined to obtain no lands from either of those nations, upon principles inconsistent with their ideas of justice and right."[54]

4.4   EQUALITY AND SLAVERY

In its final version, the U.S. Declaration of Independence boldly proclaimed:

> We hold these truths to be self-evident: that all men are created equal; that they are endowed by their Creator with certain unalienable rights; that among these rights are life, liberty, and the pursuit of happiness; that to secure these rights, governments are instituted among men...

In Enlightenment thinking, equality was inextricably connected with the concepts of Natural Law, natural rights, and liberty, and this would pose a great challenge to the Founding Fathers who, in spite of their firm belief in human equality, felt unable to abolish slavery. Like George Washington, both Jefferson and Madison owned slaves,[55] both said that they viewed the institution of slavery as an abhorrent evil, and both considered the gradual emancipation of blacks and their transfer to West Africa to be the optimal long-term solution.[56] Jefferson was convinced that, in the long term, immigrants from Europe and blacks could not live side by side in harmony. Among other things, he was convinced that deep-seated prejudices on the part of whites and deeply felt resentments on the part of blacks would be a guarantee of future interracial strife.[57] What he proposed was to introduce a program whereby children of slaves would be separated from their parents, given an education at public expense, and subsequently sent to Africa to set up their own country.[58] Madison concurred with Jefferson, believing that "existing and probably unalterable prejudices" would constitute a lasting obstacle to integration.[59]

However, Jefferson would have been unable to maintain his estate without slave labor. As he put it at one point, "Justice is in one scale, self-preservation [is] in the other."[60] Accordingly, both Jefferson and Madison favored the gradual emancipation of the slaves.[61] Madison likewise came to consider West Africa as the ideal, eventual destination for America's black population. He became involved in the American Colonization Society, an organization set up to promote this plan, and even accepted the presidency of that society.[62] Jefferson, although broadly sympathetic to the objectives of the Society, declined to join it, insisting, among other things, that slave-owners had to be financially compensated for the liberation of their slaves.[63]

Madison addressed this concern by proposing that the U.S. government use the revenues to be collected from the sale of lands in order to purchase slaves from their owners. The government would thereby free the blacks and transport them to Africa. Madison felt, nonetheless, that there might need to be exceptions: such exceptions would include those, if any, who preferred the certainties of slavery to the uncertainties of being released in a new country, as well as the disabled, the aged, or those who were simply exhausted from lifelong service. However, Madison allowed another exception, viz., that slave-owners might retain any slaves they considered too valuable to sell at prices fixed by the government.[64] To most people living in the twenty-first century, the position taken by Jefferson and Madison would seem to smack of hypocrisy; indeed, one can make an argument that, from a moral point of view, Jefferson and Madison should never have taken slaves and that, once they had slaves, they should have liberated them with financial compensation, and further that the two men should have been prepared if necessary to live out their days as working class laborers, rather than as aristocrats. That argument might impress some people as morally correct, but it is extremely hard to imagine either Jefferson or Madison renouncing their wealth out of moral concerns.

In wrestling with the problem of slavery, Jefferson and Madison were confronting head-on the most important challenge at that time to Enlightenment ideals of freedom and equality. Casting their view farther afield, Jefferson and Madison reflected on the fact that there were bright and talented children born into poor families. They were determined to give such children a chance to obtain an education and a professional career and Jefferson introduced a "bill for the more general diffusion of Knowledge" in the Virginia House of Delegates in December 1778. When it failed, Jefferson presented it again in June 1780, and Madison revived the initiative for the last time in 1786. Specifically, the bill proposed to select each year one outstanding pupil from parents of limited means, from each of roughly ten elementary schools *per county* in Virginia, to be boarded at public expense at one of the better grammar schools. There they would be taught Latin, Greek, English grammar, geography, and advanced arithmetic, with the least promising third to be dropped after one year, and only one pupil retained after the second year. The surviving pupil from each county would continue his education at public expense for another four years. With 20 counties in Virginia, this would have added up to 20 top performers graduating each year and, thereupon, being sent to the College of William and Mary, to be educated for another three years at public expense.[65]

Paine took a far more radical approach to the question of equality, calling for the immediate emancipation of all slaves and *rejecting* the idea that the conflict of interest between the natural rights of Africans in the New World (slaves) and the property "rights" (on indigenous land) of landowners should be resolved by some sort of compromise.[66] He recognized, of course, that the principle of *one man, one vote* was essential to legitimate, representative government.[67] But he took as his premise that "Public good is not a term opposed to the good of individuals. On the contrary, it is the good of every individual collected. It is the good of all, because it is the good of every one."[68] Proceeding from that premise, he outlined a radical proposal in his *Rights of Man, Part the Second* (March 1792). Among other things, he now demanded universal manhood suffrage (with no property requirement), a graduated income tax, free public education for children and adolescents, government provisions for medical care and old-age pensions,[69] and the abolition of all monarchy. Paine even suggested that people enjoyed a *natural right to welfare*[70]—a suggestion (demand) far ahead of his time and still denied in much of the world even today. In writing this, Paine echoed—whether consciously or not—Hume's 1752 *Of Commerce*, in which the Scottish philosopher had asserted that

A too great disproportion [of wealth] among the citizens weakens any state. Every person, if possible, ought to enjoy the fruits of his labour, in a full possession of all the necessaries, and many of the conveniences of life. No one can doubt, but [that] such an equality is most suitable to human nature, and diminishes much less from the happiness of the rich, than it adds to that of the poor.[71]

In support of his vision, Paine even outlined a detailed plan for taxation to fund the pensions and medical care to which he felt citizens were entitled. In writing this, Paine showed how far his thinking had evolved since his claim, in *Common Sense*, that the purpose of government could be reduced to security—or perhaps, better phrased, he had come to realize that real security includes not having to worry about whether one will have enough to eat or be able to afford medical care.

Paine would once more take up his pen to advocate greater equality for people. This he undertook in his 1795 *Agrarian Justice*,[72] in which he inquired into the origins of poverty, argued that the inequitable distribution of land violated people's natural rights, and promoted a partial redistribution of income through taxation on the more well-to-do. As he saw it, the heart of the problem was that

> Civilization has operated two ways: to make one part of society more affluent, and the other more wretched, than would have been the lot of either in a natural state...[T]he accumulation of personal property is, in many instances, the effect of paying too little for the labor that produced it; the consequence of which is that the working hand perishes in old age, and the employer abounds in affluence.[73]

Whether Paine stopped short of advocating socialism,[74] or presented a "quasi-socialist" program,[75] it is clear that Paine was a visionary and perhaps even, in the most positive sense, a pragmatic utopian.[76]

4.5 RELIGIOUS LIBERTY AND OTHER RIGHTS

That Paine and Jefferson were Deists has been widely acknowledged.[77] Deism (see Box 4.3) was neither anti-Christian nor, in the minds of its advocates, non-Christian, though it tended to be anti-clerical, in the sense of opposing ecclesiastical establishments, denying the literal truth of the Bible, and, certainly in Jefferson's case, denying both "revelation as a source of religious knowledge" generally and the doctrine of the Holy Trinity specifically.[78] For that matter, on these two points, Paine was in full agreement. James Madison, on the other hand, "was not so outspoken in his religious views," although he did admit "that his thought was influenced by the liberal ideas current at the time."[79]

Box 4.3: Deism
Deism was a belief system enjoying some subscription among intellectuals in eighteenth-century Europe and America, which held that God had created the world including humans, but then left people to their own devices. According to Deists, God did not interfere in human

affairs, which also meant that praying to God for miracles was pointless. Benjamin Franklin, Thomas Jefferson, and Thomas Paine were among the best known Deists in America at the time. Franklin and Jefferson were committed to promoting religious tolerance, while Paine's *Age of Reason* was critical of traditional Christianity.

Thomas Paine offered, by way of declaring his own profession of faith, what may serve to convey the sense of Deism. His 1794 *Age of Reason* (Part One) provided the occasion for him to declare the following:

I believe in one God, and no more...
  I believe [in] the equality of man, and I believe that religious duties consist in doing justice, loving mercy, and endeavouring to make our fellow-creatures happy....I do not believe in the creed professed by the Jewish church, by the Roman church, by the Greek church, by the Turkish church, by the Protestant church, nor by any church that I know of. My own mind is my own church.[80]

Paine had said very little about religious belief in his *Common Sense*, where he had been content to plead that government guarantee freedom of religion, declaring that he himself considered "the various denomina-tions among us, to be like children of the same family, differing only, in what is called their Christian names."[81] This plea for tolerance—at a time when ecclesiastical establishment was the rule throughout the thir-teen colonies—gave no hint of the fury he would unleash with his *Age of Reason*, Part One and, more particularly, with Part Two. Two hundred years later, Paine's argument that the books of the Old and New Testa-ment were, with some exceptions, not written by the persons whose names they bear is generally accepted by Biblical scholars. But in his time, this argument struck most of his readers as blasphemous—his internal evidence notwithstanding.[82] In addition, he gave offense to Christians by declaring (in Part Two) that one had to choose between believing in the moral justice and goodness of God and believing in the Bible.[83] But his sustained, acidic mockery of various stories in the Bible, such as the one about Jonah and the whale, may have given the most offense to his readers. It is true, to be sure, that he was not the only educated person in his time to hold such views about the Bible. For example, John Adams, counted as "the most openly Christian of the first American presidents," noted privately that he thought "that the Bible was full of 'whole cart-loads of trumpery'."[84] But Paine went public with his views, and therein lay the scandal.

Jefferson and Madison had no ambition to disabuse people of the particulars of their faith. What they wanted was to assure freedom of religious belief and practice, in the conviction that this was one of the most basic natural rights (in today's terminology, we would say *human rights*). For many people in that era (and still today, for that matter), morality was seen as dependent on religion, apparently on the supposition that, aside from self-interest,[85] the only motivations to moral behavior were obedience to the Ten Commandments (i.e., to God) and the desire for heavenly reward. Jefferson (like other intellectuals of his generation, such as Hume) disputed this linkage. He argued that people had an innate moral sense, and could understand the difference between right and wrong instinctively, which is to say without consulting either revelation or the elders in one's Church.[86] Accordingly, Jefferson argued, in his *Notes on the State of Virginia* (echoing Locke), that government could not have any authority to dictate in matters of faith and religious ritual. "The legitimate powers of government extend to such acts only as are injurious to others," he wrote there. "But it does me no injury for my neighbour to say there are twenty gods, or no god. It neither picks my pocket nor breaks my leg...Constraint may make him worse by making him a hypocrite, but it will never make him a truer man."[87] Moreover, Jefferson found the diversity of opinion positively "advantageous to religion" insofar as it fostered free inquiry, in which the various Churches could act as checks on each other.[88]

At the time of the Revolution, the Congregational (i.e., Presbyterian) Church was the established Church in New England, while the Episcopal (i.e., Anglican) Church was the established Church in the remaining states. The presence of large numbers of Quakers in Pennsylvania, Catholics in Maryland, and members of various other religious bodies throughout the thirteen emerging states created a pressure for change. Already in 1779, while the Revolutionary War was still being fought, Jefferson, at the time a member of the General Assembly of Virginia, introduced a Bill for Establishing Religious Freedom for the consideration of that body. In presenting it, Jefferson argued that "our civil rights [should] have no dependence on our religious opinions."[89] Conservatives, however, blocked it, and the Episcopal Church remained the official Church of Virginia for the time being.

Subsequently, in 1785, Patrick Henry, likewise a member of the Virginia assembly, introduced a bill to impose a general tax for the support of "Teachers of the Christian Religion." These funds were to be assigned to ministers or teachers of the Gospel or to provide for places of divine worship; however, the Quakers and Mennonites, who did not have clergy, were to be allowed to use these funds as they saw fit.[90] Madison and other progressives consulted and it was decided that Madison should prepare a comprehensive statement on the issue. The result was one of his most famous writings, his "Memorial and Remonstrance Against Religious Assessments," to which the leaders of various non-Anglican Church bodies, as well as a number of Anglican ecclesiastical dignitaries, lent their support.

Madison made several arguments in his "Memorial and Remonstrance," specifically

- that equality of religious beliefs had already been affirmed in the Virginia Declaration of Rights, while this bill would undermine that equality;
- that the bill would declare the civil magistrate competent to judge religious truth, in distinguishing those Churches worthy of receiving support from those not worthy;
- that passage of the bill would discourage immigration, upon which the newly independent states were counting;
- that the jurisdiction proposed by Patrick Henry would differ from the Inquisition only in degree, but not in fundamental character;
- that the bill would foster social disharmony; and
- that the bill would, in fact, have effects adverse to the spread of Christianity.[91]

As Garrett Ward Sheldon has pointed out, Madison's undertaking to write his "Memorial and Remonstrance" was "largely motivated by a desire to protect the [C]hurch from the corrupting influence of the state, rather than an effort to remove religion from any role in civic life."[92] This document was quickly circulated throughout the state, eliciting a torrent of petitions—roughly 90 in all—supporting Madison's arguments, but only about 10 petitions in favor of Patrick Henry's bill.[93] The effect was to kill the bill. At this point, Madison and his colleagues revived Jefferson's Bill for Establishing Religious Freedom, which was passed without substantial alteration.

As already mentioned, Madison was rather private about his religious views but it is clear that, on one particular point at least, Madison parted ways with Jefferson. This had to do with Jefferson's belief that religion could be useful in restraining people from extreme behavior. Madison's view was that, on the contrary, "even in its coolest state [religion] has been much oftener a motive to oppression than a restraint from it."[94] This assessment was, as we have already seen, reflected in Madison's paper No. 10 for *The Federalist*.

Madison went on to champion the Bill of Rights—initially with skepticism, having felt that it was unnecessary, potentially divisive, and intruding upon the prerogatives rightfully belonging to the states. But, having participated in the Constitutional Convention in Philadelphia, 1787, Madison saw that the absence of a bill of rights was already stirring opposition to the draft constitution. Alexander Hamilton, one of his collaborators in *The Federalist* papers, tried to stem the tide of opposition by arguing that

...bills of rights, in the sense and to the extent in which they are contended for, are not only unnecessary in the proposed Constitution but would even be dangerous. They would contain various exceptions to powers which are not granted; and, on this very account, would afford a colorable pretext to claim more [powers] than were granted. For why declare that things shall not be done which there is no power to do? Why, for instance, should it be said that the liberty of the press shall not be restrained, when no power is given by which restrictions may be imposed?[95]

For that matter, Madison had already made his case in *Federalist* No. 48 that the institution of representative government, with its separation of powers, would serve as a sufficient guarantee against encroachments by the authorities on people's rights, concluding that the advocates of a bill of rights were overly and unnecessarily cautious in urging people "to indulge all their jealousy and exhaust all their precautions."[96]

Before it could take effect, the constitution had to be ratified by nine of the thirteen states, which, in the years since the Revolution, had subscribed to the loose Articles of Confederation—Articles which had given rise to various difficulties. There were three possible paths now:

ratification; failure to ratify and the summoning of a fresh convention to draft a new constitution; or ratification on the pledge that a bill of rights would be added later. In early June 1788, Jefferson wrote to William Carmichael, from Paris, to endorse the plan advocated by Massachusetts, viz., to accept the constitution as it stood and amend it afterwards.[97]

By the end of May 1788, South Carolina had become the eighth state to ratify the constitution, while New Hampshire endorsed it even as the Virginia legislators were still in session debating the text. Although, with New Hampshire's ratification, the constitution came into effect for those states which had ratified it, had Virginia rejected the constitution, "the nation might have degenerated into regional confederacies...with those confederations likely forming foreign alliances."[98] At the Virginia convention, Patrick Henry warned that, in his view, the constitution would give the Congress "an unlimited, unbounded command over the soul of this Commonwealth [Virginia]," adding that it would "destroy the State governments, and swallow the liberties of the people, without giving them previous notice."[99] For his part, Jefferson was not as agitated about this issue as Henry seemed to be, but he wrote to Madison in late December to support the constitution but to persuade his colleague and friend that a bill of rights was, in fact, a good idea.

By then, Madison was reaching the same conclusion and, immediately after ratification, Madison led the way to reviewing the 40 or so amendments which had been presented at the convention, of which about half referred to rights of one kind or another.[100] Although, as Labunski notes, "Madison's 'conversion' over the bill of rights...did not happen overnight,"[101] once converted to the cause, he embraced it with alacrity. Elected to the Houses of Representatives in March 1789, he announced already on 4 May, barely a month after quorum had been achieved, that he would be presenting a set of amendments to the constitution for consideration. In addition to securing a constitutional guarantee for freedom of religion, the amendments he proposed included also guarantees for freedoms of speech and press, the right to trial by jury, the prohibition of arbitrary searches, and guarantees against excessive bail and double jeopardy.[102] Among these, Madison set particular store on the guarantee of religious liberty. Madison's draft would be revised in some details but, by 25 September 1789, the package of 12 amendments to the U.S. Constitution, known as the Bill of Rights, had been passed by both houses of Congress and, a week later, that package was submitted to the states for ratification. The third article to this Bill of Rights consisted of a single sentence: "Congress shall make no law establishing religion or prohibiting the free exercise thereof, nor shall the rights of Conscience be infringed." Other articles provided guarantees of freedoms of speech, assembly, and press, the right to be secure from "unreasonable searches and seizures," and the right to trial by jury, among other things. Passage of this set of amendments was a tremendous achievement, for which Madison deserves a large part of the credit. There was, however, one amendment, passage of which he failed to secure. While Article 3 banned any action on the part of the U.S. Congress to infringe on religious freedom, it made no provision regarding the states, which were therefore left free to make their own decisions concerning the extent of religious liberty they wished to permit. To address this dilemma, Madison had proposed an amendment that "No State shall violate the equal rights of conscience, or the freedom of the press, or the trial by jury in criminal cases."[103] Although it passed in the House, this amendment was defeated in the Senate, where defense of states' rights took priority over individual rights.

4.6   A Summing Up

Paine, Jefferson, and Madison were well versed in the ideas of the English and Scottish Enlightenments and subscribed to the notion of natural rights, championing religious and other liberties, supporting the separation of Church and state, and advocating some measure of equality (above all in Paine's case, as we have seen). In spite of their holding slaves, Jefferson and Madison were worried about what the institution of slavery would mean for the new country.

Notes

1. I have drawn this list from Shane J. Ralston, "American Enlightenment Thought", in the *Internet Encyclopedia of Philosophy*, at https://iep.utm.edu/american-enlightenment-thought/ [accessed on 6 January 2024].
2. *Ibid.*, p. 8 of 12 (emphasis added).
3. Paine never called himself "Tom"; the diminutive arose as a British Tory slur against the radical convert to American independence and anti-monarchical revolution. See Craig Nelson, *Thomas*

104 S. P. RAMET

Paine: Enlightenment, Revolution, and the Birth of Modern America (London: Penguin Books, 2006), pp. 228–229.

4. On Jefferson's friendship with Madison, see Adrienne Koch, *Jefferson and Madison: The Great Collaboration* (New York: Alfred A. Knopf, 1950). See also Andrew Burstein and Nancy Isenberg, *Madison and Jefferson* (New York: Random House, 2010).

5. A. J. Ayer, *Thomas Paine* (Chicago: University of Chicago Press, 1988), pp. 55, 187.

6. Christopher Hitchens, *Thomas Jefferson* (New York: HarperPerennial, 2005; this edition 2009), p. 44; and Noble E. Cunningham, Jr., *In Pursuit of Reason: The Life of Thomas Jefferson* (New York: Ballantine Books, 1987), pp. 18 and 197.

7. Harvey J. Kaye, *Thomas Paine and the Promise of America* (New York: Hill and Wang, 2005), pp. 50 and passim; and Nelson, *Thomas Paine*, pp. 82–83, 92–93.

8. Ayer, *Thomas Paine*, p. 120.

9. Nelson, *Thomas Paine*, p. 208.

10. See Richard Labunski, *James Madison and the Struggle for the Bill of Rights* (Oxford and New York: Oxford University Press, 2006).

11. See S. Gerald Sandler, "Lockean Ideas in Thomas Jefferson's Bill for Establishing Religious Freedom", in *Journal of the History of Ideas*, Vol. 21, No. 1 (January–March 1960), pp. 110–116.

12. As quoted in Cunningham, *In Pursuit of Reason*, p. 30.

13. As quoted in Adrienne Koch, *The Philosophy of Thomas Jefferson* (Gloucester, Mass.: Peter Smith, 1957), p. 155.

14. Cunningham, *In Pursuit of Reason*, p. 30; Joseph J. Ellis, *American Sphinx: The Character of Thomas Jefferson* (New York: Vintage Books, 1996; this edition 1998), p. 119; and Robert Ketcham, *James Madison: A Biography* (Charlottesville: University of Virginia Press, 1990), p. 86.

15. Cunningham, *In Pursuit of Reason*, pp. 30, 49; Fred C. Luebke, "The Origins of Thomas Jefferson's Anti-Clericalism", in *Church History*, Vol. 32, No. 3 (September 1963), pp. 344–345; and Dumas Malone, *Jefferson and His Time*, Vol. 2: *Jefferson and the Rights of Man* (Boston: Little, Brown & Co., 1951), p. 211.

16. Gary Rosen, *American Compact: James Madison and the Problem of Founding* (Lawrence: University Press of Kansas, 1999), p. 107; confirmed in Mark G. Spencer, "Hume and Madison on

Faction", in *The William and Mary Quarterly*, Third Series, Vol. 59, No. 4 (October 2002), pp. 869—896, especially pp. 869–870; reconfirmed in Roy Branson, "James Madison and the Scottish Enlightenment", in *Journal of the History of Ideas*, Vol. 40, No. 2 (April–June 1979), pp. 235–250.

17. Garrett Ward Sheldon, *The Political Philosophy of James Madison* (Baltimore and London: The Johns Hopkins University Press, 2001), p. 80. Regarding the influence of ancient Greek and Roman writers on Jefferson and Madison more generally, see Carl J. Richard, *The Founders and the Classics: Greece, Rome, and the American Enlightenment* (Cambridge, Mass.: Harvard University Press, 1994).

18. Letter from TJ to Peter Carr (10 August 1787), in Adrienne Koch and William Peden (eds.), *The Life and Selected Writings of Thomas Jefferson* (New York: Modern Library, 1944; this edition 2004), p. 398.

19. JM, "No. 55: The Total Number of the House of Representatives", in Alexander Hamilton, James Madison, and John Jay, *The Federalist Papers*, ed. by Clinton Rossiter (New York: New American Library—Signet Classics, 2003), p. 343.

20. JM, "No. 51: The Structure of the Government Must Furnish the Proper Checks and Balances between the Different Departments", in *Federalist Papers*, p. 319.

21. Paine, *Common Sense*, p. 68.

22. *Ibid.*, p. 65.

23. *Ibid.*, p. 98.

24. As quoted in Ayer, *Thomas Paine*, p. 85.

25. Eric Foner, *Tom Paine and Revolutionary France* (New York: Oxford University Press, 1976), p. 214, quoting from Burke's *Reflections*.

26. Letter from TJ to Joseph Priestley (27 January 1800), in Koch and Peden (eds.), *Selected Writings of Thomas Jefferson*, p. 508.

27. Letter from TJ to JM (6 September 1789), in Koch and Peden (eds.), *Selected Writings of Thomas Jefferson*, p. 451.

28. "Inaugural Address" (4 March 1801), in Koch and Peden (eds.), *Selected Writings of Thomas Jefferson*, p. 298.

29. *Ibid.*, p. 300.

30. Letter from TJ to Edward Carrington (4 August 1787), in Koch and Peden (eds.), *Selected Writings of Thomas Jefferson*, p. 395.

31. JM, "No. 47: The Particular Structure of the New Government and the Distribution of Power Among Its Different Parts", in *Federalist Papers*, p. 299.

32. JM, "No. 14: Objections to the Proposed Constitution from Extent of Territory Answered", in *Federalist Papers*, p. 95.

33. As quoted in Spencer, "Hume and Madison", p. 880.

34. JM, "No. 10: The Same Subject Continued", in *Federalist Papers*, p. 72.

35. *Ibid.*, p. 73.

36. *Ibid.*, pp. 72–73, 75, 79.

37. "The Declaration of Independence", reproduced in "The Autobiography of Thomas Jefferson", in Koch and Peden (eds.), *Selected Writings of Thomas Jefferson*, p. 24.

38. JM, "No. 40: The Powers of the Convention to Form a Mixed Government Examined and Sustained", in *Federalist Papers*, p. 249.

39. JM, "No. 51", p. 321, my emphasis.

40. Its official name was the *American* Party, but it was routinely called the Know Nothing Party in contemporary news reports and has been likewise in subsequent scholarship. See Sabrina P. Ramet and Christine M. Hassenstab, "The Know Nothing Party: Three Theories about its Rise and Demise", in *Politics and Religion*, Vol. 6 (2013), pp. 570–595.

41. Nelson, *Thomas Paine*, p. 54.

42. Kaye, *Thomas Paine*, p. 54.

43. Hitchens, *Thomas Jefferson*, pp. 151–152.

44. TJ, "First Annual Message" as President (8 December 1801), in Koch and Peden (eds.), *Selected Writings of Thomas Jefferson*, p. 302. See also Peter S. Onuf, *The Mind of Thomas Jefferson* (Charlottesville, Va.: University of Virginia Press, 2007), pp. 220, 259.

45. TJ, "Second Inaugural Address" (4 March 1805), in Koch and Peden (eds.), *Selected Writings of Thomas Jefferson*, p. 315.

46. Roger Kennedy, "Jefferson and the Indians", in *Winterthur Portfolio*, Vol. 27, No. 2/3 (Summer–Autumn 1992), p. 105.

47. As quoted in Ellis, *American Sphinx*, p. 240. For further discussion, see also Anthony F. C. Wallace, *Jefferson and the Indians: The Tragic Fate of the First Americans* (Cambridge, Mass.: The Belknap Press of Harvard University Press, 1999).

48. Michael Witgen, "A Nation of Settlers: The Early American Republic and the Colonization of the Northwest Territory", in *The William and Mary Quarterly*, Vol. 76, No. 3 (July 2019), pp. 391, 394, 397.
49. JM, "No. 42: The Powers Conferred by the Constitution Further Considered", in *Federalist Papers*, p. 265.
50. Letter from JM to James Monroe (27 November 1784), *The Founders' Constitution*, at http://press-pubs.uchicago.edu/founders/documents/a1_8_3_indianss2.html [accessed on 23 February 2011].
51. Letter from JM to James Monroe (24 December 1784), *familytales*, at http://www.familytales.org/dbDisplay.php?id=ltr_mad 1509 [accessed on 23 February 2011].
52. Irving Brant's paraphrase, in *The Fourth President: A Life of James Madison* (Indianapolis: Bobbs-Merrill, 1970), p. 405.
53. *Ibid.*, pp. 512—513.
54. As quoted in *Ibid.*, p. 596.
55. The Madison family owned 118 slaves in 1782, while Jefferson owned 167 slaves in 1796. Ketcham, *James Madison*, p. 12 and Ellis, *American Sphinx*, p. 171.
56. Cunningham, *In Pursuit of Reason*, p. 61; and Robert A. Dahl, "James Madison: Republican or Democrat?", in *Perspectives on Politics*, Vol. 3, No. 3 (September 2005), p. 445.
57. Ellis, *American Sphinx*, p. 174.
58. Ari Helo and Peter Onuf, "Jefferson, Morality, and the Problem of Slavery", in *The William and Mary Quarterly*, Third Series, Vol. 60, No. 3 (July 2003), p. 584. See also Nancy V. Morrow, "The Problem of Slavery in the Polemic Literature of the American Enlightenment", in *Early American Literature*, Vol. 20, No. 3 (Winter 1985/1986), p. 250.
59. JM, as quoted in Ketcham, *James Madison*, p. 625.
60. As quoted in C. Vann Woodward, "A Few Words About Jefferson and Madison on Slavery", in *The Journal of Blacks in Higher Education*, No. 9 (Autumn 1995), p. 50.
61. Regarding Jefferson's attempt to include a reference to African slaves in his initial draft for the *Declaration of Independence*, a reference removed by the Continental Congress, see Edwin Gittleman, "Jefferson's 'Slave Narrative': The Declaration of Independence as a Literary Text", in *Early American Literature*, Vol. 8, No. 3 (Winter 1974), p. 251.

S. P. RAMET

63. Onuf, *The Mind*, pp. 221—223.
64. Edward McNall Burns, *James Madison: Philosopher of the Constitution*, new ed. (New York: Octagon Books, 1968), pp. 77–78.
65. Cunningham, *In Pursuit of Reason*, p. 59.
66. Morrow, "The Problem of Slavery", pp. 252–253.
67. Thomas Paine, *Dissertation on First Principles of Government* (1795), in Michael Foot and Isaac Kramnick (eds.), *The Thomas Paine Reader* (London: Penguin Books, 1987), p. 459.
68. As quoted in Foner, *Tom Paine and Revolutionary America*, p. 87.
69. The provisions for coverage of medical care and old-age pensions are detailed in Thomas Paine, *The Rights of Man*, Part Two (1792), in Thomas Paine, *The Rights of Man*, with an introduction by Eric Foner (Harmondsworth: Penguin Books, 1985), chap. 5 (pp. 210—273).
70. John W. Seaman, "Thomas Paine: Ransom, Civil Peace, and the Natural Right to Welfare", in *Political Theory*, Vol. 16, No. 1 (February 1988), pp. 120—121.
71. As quoted in Nelson, *Thomas Paine*, p. 218.
72. Thomas Paine, *Agrarian Justice, Opposed to Agrarian Law, and to Agrarian Monopoly* (Philadelphia: Printed by R. Folwell for Benjamin Franklin Bache, 1797?).
73. As quoted in Kaye, *Thomas Paine and the Promise*, p. 86.
74. Nelson, *Thomas Paine*, p. 290.
75. Paul F. Beller, "Thomas Paine and Natural Rights: A Reconsideration", in *Social Science*, Vol. 52, No. 2 (Spring 1977), pp. 69–70.
76. See Mark Jendrysik, "Tom Paine: Utopian?", in *Utopian Studies*, Vol. 18, No. 2 (2007), pp. 139–157.
77. Regarding Jefferson, see Ellis, *American Sphinx*, pp. 309—310; Onuf, *The Mind*, pp. 146–148; Daniel J. Boorstin, *The Lost World of Thomas Jefferson* (New York: Henry Holt, 1948), passim; and Malone, *Jefferson and His Time*, p. 111.
78. George Harmon Knoles,"The Religious Ideas of Thomas Jefferson", in Merrill D. Peterson (ed.), *Thomas Jefferson: A Profile* (New York: Hill and Wang, 1967), pp. 243–260, at pp. 245, 251.

79. William Warren Sweet,"Natural Religion and Religious Liberty", in *The Journal of Religion*, Vol. 25, No. 1 (January 1945), p. 53.
80. Thomas Paine, *The Age of Reason, Being an Investigation of True and Fabulous Theology*, ed. by Moncure Daniel Conway (Mineola, N.Y.: Dover Publications, 2004), pp. 21–22.
81. Paine, *Common Sense*, p. 109.
82. For that matter, Benedict de Spinoza (1632–1677) had previously pointed out that "the Pentateuch, supposedly written by Moses, contains a description of Moses' death and of events that took place afterward." – Michael della Rocca, *Spinoza* (London and New York: Routledge, 2008), pp. 243—244.
83. Paine, *The Age of Reason*, p. 90.
84. Nelson, *Thomas Paine*, p. 264, quoting Adams.
85. Jefferson realized that self-interest could constrain behavior, but did not believe that it could furnish a foundation for morality as such.
86. Letter from TJ to Thomas Law (13 June 1814), in Koch and Peden (eds.), *Selected Writings of Thomas Jefferson*, pp. 584–585.
87. Thomas Jefferson, *Notes on the State of Virginia*, ed. by William Peden (New York: W. W. Norton, 1954), p. 159.
88. *Ibid.*, p. 160.
89. As quoted in Hitchens, *Thomas Jefferson*, p. 36.
90. Vincent Phillip Munoz, "James Madison's Principle of Religious Liberty", in *American Political Science Review*, Vol. 97, No. 1 (February 2003), p. 21.
91. JM, "Memorial and Remonstrance against Religious Assessments" (June 1785), in *The Papers of James Madison: Vol. 8, 10 March 1784–28 March 1786*, ed. by Robert A. Rutland and William M. E. Rachal, with Barbara D. Ripel and Frederika J. Teute (Chicago and London: University of Chicago Press, 1973), pp. 295–306.
92. As paraphrased in Sarah A. Morgan Smith, "James Madison, Religious Liberty and Union", in *History of Political Thought*, Vol. 39, No. 4 (Winter 2018), p. 694.
93. Thomas S. Kidd, *God of Liberty: A Religious History of the American Revolution* (New York: Basic Books, 2010), p. 184.
94. Letter from JM to TJ (24 October 1787), as quoted in Thomas Lindsay, "James Madison on Religion and Politics: Rhetoric and

Reality", in *American Political Science Review*, Vol. 85, No. 4 (December 1991), p. 1324.
95. Alexander Hamilton, "No. 84: Certain General and Miscellaneous Objections to the Constitution Considered and Answered", in *Federalist Papers*, p. 513.
96. JM, "No. 48: These Departments Should Not Be So Far Separated as to Have No Constitutional Control over Each Other", in *Federalist Papers*, p. 306.
97. Letter from TJ to William Carmichael (3 June 1788), as cited in Labunski, *James Madison and the Struggle*, p. 59.
98. Labunski, *James Madison and the Struggle*, p. 60.
99. As quoted in *Ibid.*, p. 61.
100. *Ibid.*, pp. 108, 114.
101. *Ibid.*, p. 161.
102. *Ibid.*, p. 199.
103. As quoted in *Ibid.*, p. 259.

FURTHER READING

Burstein, Andrew and Nancy Isenberg. *Madison and Jefferson* (Random House, 2010).
Ferguson, Robert. *The American Enlightenment, 1750–1820* (Harvard University Press, 1997).
Foner, Eric. *Tom Paine and Revolutionary America* (Oxford University Press, 1976).
Helo, Ari and Peter Onuf. "Jefferson, Morality, and the Problem of Slavery", in *The William and Mary Quarterly*, Third Series, Vol. 60, No. 3 (July 2003).
Jendrysik, Mark. "Tom Paine: Utopian?", in *Utopian Studies*, Vol. 18, No. 2 (2007).
Koch, Adrienne. *The Philosophy of Thomas Jefferson* (Peter Smith, 1957).
Lamb, Robert. "The Liberal Cosmopolitanism of Thomas Paine", in *The Journal of Politics*, Vol. 76, No. 3 (July 2014).
Nelson, Craig. *Thomas Paine: Enlightenment, Revolution, and the Birth of Modern America* (Penguin, 2006).
Rich, Adrienne. *Jefferson and Madison: The Great Collaboration* (Alfred A. Knopf, 1950).
Rosen, Gary. *American Compact: James Madison and the Problem of Founding* (University Press of Kansas, 1999).

Sandler, S. Gerald. "Lockean Ideas in Thomas Jefferson's Bill for Establishing Religious Freedom", in *Journal of the History of Ideas*, Vol. 21, No. 1 (January–March 1960).

Wallace, Anthony F. C. *Jefferson and the Indians: The Tragic Fate of the First Americans* (Cambridge, Mass.: The Belknap Press of Harvard University Press, 1999).

CHAPTER 5

Mary Wollstonecraft

Sabrina P. Ramet

Abstract Best known for her *Vindication of the Rights of Woman*, Wollstonecraft was part of a radical milieu advocating the social and political transformation of Great Britain. She promoted both gender equality and greater class equality and developed theories for the education of children. Her writings have had a huge influence on subsequent advocates of women's rights, especially in her native England and in the United States.

Keywords Rights of women · Rights of men · Reason · Morality · Education of daughters · Reign of Terror · French Revolution · Slave trade · Moral corruption

Mary Wollstonecraft (1759–1797) argued that the balance of power and rights between women and men in her time violated the most obvious Enlightenment tenets of Reason and Morality and was among the first writers to point out that confining classical liberal demands for liberty and equality to men involved internal self-contradiction. It followed that consistent liberalism entailed, of necessity, feminism. She was also the first writer to associate the enslavement of (British, in this case) women with the enslavement of Africans. And she was one of the first writers to point

© The Author(s), under exclusive license to Springer Nature   113
Switzerland AG 2024
S. P. Ramet and T. L. Knutsen, *Key Thinkers of the English, Scottish and American Enlightenments*,
https://doi.org/10.1007/978-3-031-62454-4_5

out that the social and economic inequalities produced by capitalism were in a state of tension with liberal proclamations of human equality.

Her works on pedagogical, social, and political issues include: *Thoughts on the Education of Daughters, with Reflections on Female Conduct* (1787); *The Female Reader; or Miscellaneous Pieces in Prose and Verse; Selected from the Best Writers, and Disposed Under Proper Heads; for the Improvement of Young Women* (1789); *A Vindication of the Rights of Men* (1790); *A Vindication of the Rights of Woman* (1792); and *An Historical and Moral View of the Origin and Progress of the French Revolution* (1794).

This chapter focuses on her *Vindication of the Rights of Men* and her *Vindication of the Rights of Woman*—her two most influential works—while taking into account also her reconsideration of the French Revolution, as reflected in her *Historical and Moral View of the Origin and Progress of the French Revolution*.

5.1   HER LIFE AND CAREER, TO 1789

Born in London on 27 April 1759, she moved with her family to a farm at Epping when she was four. After living in two other locations, she returned to the city of her birth in 1774, but by 1784 had taken up residence in the village of Newington Green, where she attempted to set up a school for young women. In Newington Green, she was introduced to Dr. Richard Price, a Dissenting minister who was in correspondence with Joseph Priestley, the Marquis de Condorcet, Benjamin Franklin, and Thomas Jefferson, among other distinguished philosophers, scientists, and public figures.[1] Price's *Observations on the Nature of Civil Liberty, the Principles of Government, and the Justice and Policy of the War with America* had been published in 1776 and had sold more than 60,000 copies within its first year in print.[2]

As an emerging educator, she read John Locke's *Some Thoughts Concerning Education* (1693), which influenced her own pedagogical thinking. She also read various writings by David Hume, Adam Smith, William Robertson, Gottfried Wilhelm Leibniz, Immanuel Kant, Johann Kaspar Lavater, and Jean-Jacques Rousseau, for the last of whom she felt, initially, vast admiration.[3] In addition, she also read James Burgh's sundry writings on education, which devoted but little attention to the education of girls. Formulating her own ideas on the subject, she penned her first book, *Thoughts on the Education of Daughters*, in 1786; the book, which reflected a rather orthodox religious viewpoint, was published the following year. Among other things, Wollstonecraft advised girls against cosmetics, card-playing, and early marriage, and warned against the ill effects she associated with learning by rote and "premature" reading of Scripture.[4] She also lambasted the limitation on career choices for women, who, if they did not stay home to take care of their husbands and children, were typically expected to be schoolteachers, governesses, or "companions." In fact, after the collapse of her school, she abandoned teaching and became a governess in Lady Kingsborough's household. She was dismissed from this employment before the end of 1787.

She turned to writing to earn an income, translating Jacques Necker's *De l'importance des opinions religieuses* (1788) and producing a semi-autobiographical novel, *Mary, A Fiction*; both her translation and her novel were published in 1788. Other translations followed. Her publisher, Joseph Johnson, launched a journal, *The Analytical Review*, together with Thomas Christie in May 1788, and Wollstonecraft contributed a series of reviews, among others of a book about the enslavement of Africans.[5] The following year saw the publication of her *Female Reader*, a compilation of works of prose and verse intended to give its readers a basic educational foundation in literature, culture, and Scripture, accompanied by some suggested guidelines for personal conduct and behavior.[6]

Shortly after the publication of *Thoughts on the Education of Daughters*, Johnson invited her to move in with him. In exchange for lodging, she would assist with the work of the *Review*, of which she became assistant editor in 1790. Their relationship was nonsexual, but they became the best of friends. Insofar as Johnson's print shop was a meeting place for local radicals, Wollstonecraft was now afforded the opportunity to converse in a casual setting with Price, Priestley, and other free thinkers. She, along with others in this radical circle, welcomed the outbreak of the French Revolution in July 1789 and, indeed, had been sensitive enough to the rumblings in France to have anticipated it.

5.2 YEARS OF POLITICAL ENGAGEMENT, 1790–1797

In 1790, Edmund Burke (1729–1797), a Member of Parliament from 1780 to 1794, brought out his *Reflections on the Revolution in France*.[7] In these *Reflections*, Burke, who had previously applauded the American Revolution, condemned the Revolution in France, declaring reason a less reliable guide to progress than the accumulated wisdom of the past (!)

and revolution a less sure and riskier strategy for political betterment than gradual reform. Directing his vitriol against Price, Burke seemed to revel in a static vision of society, affirming at one point that the English people "know we have made no discoveries in morality. We know that no discoveries are to be made."[8] Not content with defending monarchy, aristocracy, and tradition, Burke reviled the way the French Revolution was mobilizing women into politics, declaring that women should remain passive, silent, and subordinate to men. It is worth stressing that, at the time of Burke's choleric denunciation, the French Revolution was in its most moderate phase, with a constitutional monarchy in place. He also directed some of his barbs at radical clubs in London, thereby giving personal offense to Johnson and his circle.

English radicals were scandalized by this attack on a revolution which promised liberty, equality, and fraternity; Joseph Johnson approached Wollstonecraft, whose writing talent he appreciated, and asked her if she would like to compose a reply. The result was her *Vindication of the Rights of Men*, written at great speed and in print before the end of November 1790 scarcely a month after the appearance of Burke's *Reflections*. Published anonymously, the first edition sold out within a matter of weeks, and a second edition was available already in January 1791, this time identifying Wollstonecraft as the author. Her reply (discussed at greater length below) made use of Hume's *History of England* to make the case that the laws of England had been adopted to meet time-bound challenges and contingencies and ought not, therefore, to be viewed as "...the product of...the wisdom of the ages." She further argued "...that only those institutions which could withstand the scrutiny of reason and be shown to be in conformity with natural rights and God's justice merited respect and obedience."[9]

Thomas Paine's reply to Burke (discussed in the previous chapter) appeared soon after Wollstonecraft's and the two critics of Burke came to be associated in the public mind. In September 1791, the two met for the first time, over dinner at Johnson's; this was also the occasion for her to make the acquaintance of William Godwin, whom she would eventually marry five-and-a-half years later and who was, at the time, engaged in the composition of his *Political Justice*[10] (see Box 5.1).

Box 5.1: William Godwin
William Godwin (1756–1836), English philosopher, political journalist, and religious dissenter, was born in Wisbech on the Isle of Ely. He was the son of a dissenting minister, but in his adulthood gravitated toward Deism. His major work was *An Enquiry Concerning Political Justice, and Its Influence on General Virtue and Happiness* (1793). Here he argued that government perpetuated people's ignorance and put people in a position of dependence; to remedy these diagnosed problems, he offered a vision of direct cooperation among people, which has been interpreted as having an anarchist character. He believed that utility should serve as the exclusive guide to moral action, and stressed the importance of equality, virtue, private conscience, and rights.

More than a decade earlier, the utilitarian philosopher and social reformer Jeremy Bentham (1748–1832), famous for his slogan "the greatest good for the greatest number," had criticized the virtual enslavement of women and had demanded that women be granted the right to vote and to hold office in the legislative and executive branches of the government.[11] In France, Condorcet had made much the same argument. Now, with Johnson's encouragement, Wollstonecraft lent her voice to this cause. Within six weeks she had finished *Vindication of the Rights of Woman* (1792), the book which made her the most famous woman in England—indeed, according to Barbara Taylor, the most famous female writer of her time.[12] This second book took aim especially at the Genevan philosopher Jean-Jacques Rousseau (1712–1778).

With only one exception, reviews of her *Vindication* were positive. Interestingly enough, however, most reviewers treated it as a work devoted to female education and passed over its political implications in silence.[13] The sole negative assessment appeared in *The Critical Review*, whose rapporteur appreciated more fully than the liberal reviewers the revolutionary implications of the book, rejecting Wollstonecraft's contention that women were intellectually on a par with men as well as her demand that women be represented in parliament.[14] The volume became a best-seller and would have huge influence among the emerging feminists in Britain and the United States for at least half a century. *Vindication of the Rights of Woman* was soon republished in the United States; a French translation was available before the end of the year.[15]

After the Reign of Terror, the September 1792 massacre, the Jacobin revolution the following year, and the execution of King Louis XVI also in 1793, Wollstonecraft's enthusiasm for the French Revolution dimmed. In a letter "on the Present Character of the French Nation" (1793), she expressed concern lest the aristocracy of birth be replaced by an aristocracy of wealth, which she feared would involve little or no improvement as regards either public morality or governance.[16] She had visited Paris already in 1792, and returned there for a short stay in 1794, and was aghast at the effects of the suspension of law on the behavior of the citizens of France.[17] That latter year saw the publication of her *Historical and Moral View of the Origins and Progress of the French Revolution*. In this work, she sounded distinctly more cautious than she had in her reply to Burke, even seeming to draw closer to his point of view by endorsing the need for moderation and caution in politics and advocating gradual reform. "The revolutions of states," she wrote now, "ought to be gradual; for during violent or material changes it is not so much the wisdom of measures, as the popularity they acquire…which gives them success. Men are most easily led away by the ingenious arguments, that dwell on the equality of man…."[18] She still viewed the aspirations of the French revolutionaries as meritorious, contending that the revolution reflected the society's intellectual improvement, but at the same time warned that the "[d]egeneracy of morals, with polished manners, produces the worst of passions, which floating through the social body, the genial current of natural feelings has been poisoned; and committing crimes with trembling inquietude, the culprits have not only drawn on themselves the vengeance of the law, but thrown an odium on their nature, that has blackened the face of humanity."[19] But, in her view, the promising, if misguided in some ways, Revolution of 1789–1792 had taken a bad turn in 1793. She nonetheless looked to a future when there would be a return to the ideals of the French Revolution—*liberté, egalité, fraternité*—fulfilling the promise of the Revolution in practice.[20] Indeed, in her judgment, "…out of this chaotic mass a fairer government is rising than has ever shed the sweets of social life on the world."[21] But that, she believed, would take time; in the interim, she predicted a hard passage, writing that "Europe will probably be, for some years to come, in a state of anarchy."[22] As for the French Revolution, its leaders were guilty not only of immoderation and breaches of the moral law, but also of lack of "practical knowledge" of how to run a state—which is to say, of *incompetence!*[23] This was to be her final word on the French Revolution.

In spite of her literary successes and the admiration of people she respected highly, she was suffering from recurrent bouts of depression and, in May 1795, made a bungled attempt to commit suicide. A subsequent four-month sojourn in Scandinavia[24] seemed to revive her, but, in October, having returned to England, she made a second attempt at suicide, jumping off Putney Bridge in west London. The attempt failed and she was fished out of the Thames about 200 yards downstream.[25] The following April she visited Godwin, marrying him in March 1797 and giving birth on 30 August to their daughter—Mary Wollstonecraft Godwin, better known as Mary Shelley, author of the novel, *Frankenstein*. On 10 September 1797, Wollstonecraft died of septicaemia; she was buried in St. Pancras churchyard five days later.

5.3   Vindication of the Rights of Men

The point of this section is to come to understand what Wollstonecraft made of Burke's *Reflections*, not to come to an understanding of Burke as such. Written in the form of a letter to Edmund Burke, the *Vindication of the Rights of Men* bristles with outrage. Accusing the author of *Reflections* of having incarnated "the latent spirit of tyranny," Wollstonecraft defined her stance as defending "a degree of liberty, civil and religious, as is compatible with the liberty of every other individual with whom he is united in a social compact, and the continued existence of that compact."[26]

Wollstonecraft believed that Burke stood for property and privilege, and countered that the capitalist system as it existed in England was oppressing working class people.[27] As she read Burke, he was defending the entitlement of the propertied classes to their property, regardless how they came into possession of it, she objected that "[t]he only security of property that nature authorizes and reason sanctions is, the right a man has to enjoy the acquisitions which his talents and industry have acquired; and to bequeath them to whom he chooses."[28] Where the author of *Reflections* "settle[d] slavery on an everlasting foundation," as Wollstonecraft put it, and preferred that "the slave trade ought never to be abolished" (in Wollstonecraft's paraphrase of Burke's argument), she replied that the slave trade "outrages every suggestion of reason and religion" and asked "is it not consonant with justice, with the common principles of humanity, not to mention Christianity, to abolish this abominable mischief?"[29] And where he thought political decisions should be guided—in Wollstonecraft's mock paraphrase—by "the infallible wisdom of our ancestors," she urged that reason be the arbiter in both political and private life, offering her view that reason needed to be cultivated, promising that the cultivation of reason would, in turn, be conducive to the development of virtue—presumably both in the public sphere and in the private.[30] What was at stake, as the title of her work makes explicit, was *rights*. For Burke, one might establish the rights enjoyed by humankind only—as Wollstonecraft understood him—by tracing them back in time to their original grant.[31] By contrast, for her, it was through our reason that we could understand our duties and our rights and, on this basis, she argued that, "as rational creatures," people enjoyed inherent, God-given natural rights.[32] Moreover, in what she intended as a *coup de grace*, she declared that Burke's *Reflections* "contain[ed] no reasoned argument at all." Burke's essay was, on the contrary, "merely an expression of Burke's obsessive vanity," revealing his craving for public attention.[33]

The most basic rights, she believed, were the rights to liberty (within the limits specified above) and equality, which she saw as conjoined with virtue (respect for the moral law) to form a symbiotic triad.[34] Indeed, in her view, liberty without equality was nonsense: the former entailed the latter. Moral liberty is, at the same time, conjoined with virtue since only a person who makes her own decisions for herself can develop and cultivate virtue.[35] Wollstonecraft believed (as Kant did) that people had a duty to cultivate virtue, and she argued, in her reply to Burke, that government should encourage the development of virtue, both civic and private.[36]

Now, if equality was essential to both liberty and virtue, then it followed that the inequality of rank, wealth, and property which Burke championed was not only an affront to justice, at least as Wollstonecraft understood it, but also the seedbed for the moral corruption of society. "Virtue can only flourish amongst equals," she replied.[37] This was why the success of the Revolution—not just in France but throughout Europe—mattered, if the traditional hierarchical structure, underpinned by the patriarchal family, was to be supplanted by a more moral social and political order. Until then, the patriarchal family would continue to serve its social function as "a cesspool of vice, not a cradle of virtue."[38] Wollstonecraft was utterly consistent in her outrage at slavery and her commitment to equality, thus supporting the abolitionist cause. Looking beyond the customary concerns of most English at that time, she also called for the indigenous people of the New World to be treated as fellow human beings, invested with basic human rights.[39]

In spite of its brevity, Gary Kelly has described *A Vindication of the Rights of Men* as "a considerable achievement." As he notes,

> Not only did Wollstonecraft take on the most celebrated political orator and writer of the day, and the man who set the terms of the British debate on the French Revolution, but she engaged with both the central themes and the rhetorical strategy of the *Reflections*...At the same time, she emphasized the major role of gender in the struggle of class and culture.[40]

Not surprisingly, the volume excited a great deal of attention, both laudatory and critical.[41]

5.4   Vindication of the Rights of Woman

Wollstonecraft's concerns embraced not just female equality but also class equality, civic virtue, education, and—as already noted—the triad, liberty, equality, and virtue (which is to say, moral behavior). Yet today she is remembered largely for her defense of the rights of women. She was not the first to take up this cause. One may recall the contributions of Cristina da Pizzano (1364–c. 1430); closer to Wollstonecraft's time, one might mention Bathsua Makin's *An Essay to Revive the Antient Education of Gentlewomen, in religion, manners, arts & tongues* (1673), Mary Astell's *Serious Proposal to the Ladies, for the Advancement of Their True and Greatest Interest* (1694), and *Woman Not Inferior to Man: Or a Short and Modest Vindication of the Natural Right of the Fair-Sex to a Perfect Equality of Power, Dignity, and Esteem* (1739), a work signed by "Sophia, Person of Quality" and traditionally attributed to Lady Mary Wortley Montagu.[42] Moreover, after the publication of a condescending reply by an anonymous "Gentleman," "Sophia" responded with her *Woman's Superior Excellence to Man* (1740). In her own day, her contribution to the debate was preceded by the publication in 1790 of Olympe de Gouges's *A Declaration of the Rights of Woman*. If Wollstonecraft was not, by any stretch of the imagination, the first to advocate either the education of women or gender equality, her *Vindication of the Rights of Woman* [VRW] nonetheless had a greater impact than any of those taking up the fight previously. This may be attributed, in part, to the political context in which she wrote: in a word, the Western world was ripe for her message and there was a radical audience predisposed to read her plea with sympathy. Second, with her reply to Burke, she had already established an international reputation, so that potential readers would have a heightened interest in what *she* had to say on the subject. Third, although the book shows her indebtedness to Locke, Helvétius, and, for that matter, Rousseau, among others, her central argument—that keeping women in a position of inferiority would retard the progress of civiliza-tion—was original.[43] And finally, as her biographer Ralph Wardle put it, "…despite its discursiveness and its artificialities, *The Rights of Woman* is a great book."[44]

As with her reply to Burke, VRW was driven by outrage—with Jean-Jacques Rousseau serving as her main adversary. Her litany of criticisms of the Genevan philosopher was extensive. For example, she accused him, in his alleged nostalgia for life before the establishment of political communities, of celebrating "barbarism."[45] Again, she rejected Rousseau's notion that there were different standards of virtue for women and men, urging that the latter should learn to become "more chaste and modest."[46] She objected strenuously to his supposition that women were inferior in rational capacity and drew the inference that, if women may be shown to have equal rational ability with men, then there is no reason to exclude women from political participation on an equal basis with men.[47] And she bridled, inevitably, at Rousseau's desire to keep women "weak and passive," to train them to believe it was their duty to make themselves "agreeable" to men (while men were not expected to be agreeable to women!), and to educate girls and boys differently in order not merely to reinforce what Rousseau considered to be the different characters of the sexes, but even to create artificial differences between women and men.[48] In Wollstonecraft's view, girls and boys should be educated *together* and receive equal education. Ideally, she hoped that a reformed system of education would not only promote gender equality, but also serve to reduce class inequality.[49] She saw clearly that women's expectations, suppositions, and behaviors had been warped by patriarchal society, among other things through "a false system of education" which persuaded women to accept a subordinate status and role.[50]

Much of Rousseau's thinking about gender relations is encapsulated in his book *Emile*. Here he argued, among other things, that "[v]ague assertions as to the equality of the sexes and the similarity of their duties are only empty words," and further, that "the law of nature bids woman to obey the man."[51] Rousseau took this argument as far as urging that women had no right to refuse their husbands, when the latter demanded sexual pleasure.[52] Not surprisingly, Rousseau held that a woman's mind should be "pleasing but not brilliant, and thorough but not deep."[53] Thus, from Rousseau's point of view, women's subjection to men was entirely rational.[54]

Receiving less education than men and socialized to accept an inferior status, the women in Wollstonecraft's time were "enfeebled by false refinement" and kept in something akin to "a state of perpetual childhood."[55] The inequality of the sexes was manifested, among other places, in the family. Where Burke had argued that love precluded respect[56] and where Rousseau had sought to socialize women to accept that their subordination to their husbands was in harmony with higher principles of the universe, Wollstonecraft called for marriage to be based on friendship and mutual respect, which she understood would provide the firmest assurance of genuine affection in the relationship.[57] Rousseau's philosophy of education she characterized as "a doctrine pregnant with mischief and derogatory to the character of supreme wisdom."[58]

What was needed, she counseled, was nothing less than "a revolution in female manners"[59]—which is to say a revolution in the way women thought of themselves. In order for that to work, she realized, a revolution in men's thinking would also be required. Although, in her last essay ("On Poetry"), she bemoaned the slowness with which societies were advancing in understanding and political wisdom,[60] she appreciated, nonetheless, that it would "require a considerable length of time to eradicate the firmly rooted prejudices" about relations between the sexes.[61] Yet she sounded an optimistic note in VRW, holding that "as sound politics diffuse liberty, mankind, including woman, will become more wise and virtuous."[62]

Unmistakably rooted in the radical wing of the liberal Enlightenment, her *Vindication* offered a perspective missing in, let us say, Locke or Rousseau. As Wardle has rightly noted, Wollstonecraft's "...religion and ethics, her educational theories, and her philosophy never followed the conventional patterns of her era, nor did they adhere to the theories adopted by the radical group with whom she associated. [She] was unconventional even in her liberalism."[63]

5.5   WOLLSTONECRAFT'S IMPACT AND IMPORTANCE

As with the other thinkers discussed herein, the four central themes of the Enlightenment loomed large for Wollstonecraft. She appealed to Reason and Morality in the first place in her critique of Burke and Rousseau, although she generally used the term *Virtue*, where the others wrote of Natural Law, because, like Kant, she thought of morality a dimension not just of institutions and traditions, but also of individual and group behavior. Like all the Enlightenment thinkers, she linked Rights, Morality, and Equality but, unlike mainstream thinkers of the Enlightenment, she extended the demand for equality not only to men of means, as in Burke's case, or to men in general, as in Rousseau's case, or to men of property, as in the case of Jefferson and Madison, or to European men, as in the case of Locke, who defended the supposed right of European immigrants to seize land in the New World inhabited by indigenous nations, but also to property-less men, slaves, women—in fact, everyone. And, as we have seen, she considered the patriarchal family, which held women in subjection, "a cesspool of vice."

A thinker's importance may be measured by the originality of her ideas, by the comprehensiveness of her vision, and by her impact on her own generation as well as on succeeding generations. On all three of these criteria, Wollstonecraft may be counted as a major thinker, and, when it comes to her impact, there can be no doubt of the significance of her contribution to Western political thought. Virginia Sapiro has quite rightly called Wollstonecraft a "visionary political thinker."[64]

Although her works have been translated into several languages (among them, German, French, Portuguese, Spanish, Italian, Serbian, Polish, Norwegian, and Swedish), her impact has been greatest in the English-speaking world. In her native Britain, her work influenced and encouraged such advocates of women's rights as Mary Hays, Amelia Opie, Harriet Taylor, John Stuart Mill, and Millicent Garrett Fawcett, among others.[65] Nineteenth-century American feminists such as Frances Wright, Margaret Fuller, Hannah Mather Crocker, Lucretia Mott, Elizabeth Cady Stanton, and Susan B. Anthony admired Wollstonecraft greatly and were indebted to her.[66] Her ideas also contributed to shaping the mindsets of Romantic writers such as Lord Byron, Samuel Coleridge, William Wordsworth, and Mary and Percy Shelley. Nor should one omit to mention her influence on Welsh socialist Robert Owen and on the Russian-born anarchist Emma Goldman.[67]

In addition to what has already been noted above, it should be acknowledged that she pressed for the reform of divorce laws in England in order to give women equal rights with men in suing for divorce, advocated the end of the practice of leaving the property of an estate exclusively to the eldest son, promoted physical exercise for infants and young children, and worked to establish a national system of co-educational state schools in Britain.[68] Finally, although she was not the first to champion women's rights, her writing had an impact which previous writings on the subject had not had. Engaged with the issues of her day, Wollstonecraft understood more clearly than many of her day that the classical liberal commitment to human equality was an empty promise unless it included women.

NOTES

1. Claire Tomalin, *The Life and Death of Mary Wollstonecraft* (London: Penguin Books, 1974, 1992), pp. 45–46.
2. Ralph M. Wardle, *Mary Wollstonecraft: A Critical Biography* (London and Lawrence, Kansas: The Richards Press and the University of Kansas Press, 1951; 2nd printing, 1952), pp. 32–33.
3. Sylvana Tomaselli, "Introduction" to Mary Wollstonecraft, *A Vindication of the Rights of Men* and *A Vindication of the Rights of Woman* [hereafter, *Vindications*], ed. by Sylvana Tomaselli (Cambridge: Cambridge University Press, 1995; reprinted 2001), pp. xiii, xvi; and Tomalin, *The Life*, pp. 53–54.
4. Tomalin, *The Life*, pp. 57–58; and Barbara Taylor, *Mary Wollstonecraft and the Feminist Imagination* (Cambridge: Cambridge University Press, 2003), p., 95.
5. Moira Ferguson, "Mary Wollstonecraft and the Problematic of Slavery", in *Feminist Review*, No. 42 (Autumn 1992), pp. 83–84. See also Taylor, *Mary Wollstonecraft*, p. 240.
6. Moira Ferguson, "The Discovery of Mary Wollstonecraft's'The Female Reader'", in *Signs*, Vol. 3, No. 4 (Summer 1978), pp. 945–957, especially pp. 946–947.
7. Edmund Burke, *Reflections on the Revolution in France, and on the Proceedings of Certain Societies in London Relative to That Event* (London: J. Dodsley, 1790).

8. *Ibid.*, as quoted in David Bromwich, "Wollstonecraft as a Critic of Burke", in *Political Theory*, Vol. 23, No. 4 (November 1995), p. 626.

9. Tomaselli, "Introduction", p. xxiv.

10. William Godwin, *Enquiry Concerning Political Justice, and Its Influence on Morals and Happiness*, 2nd ed. corrected, 2 vols. (London: Printed for G. G. and J. Robinson, 1796).

11. Miriam Williford, "Bentham on the Rights of Women", in *Journal of the History of Ideas*, Vol. 36, No. 1 (January-March 1975), pp. 167–168.

12. Taylor, *Mary Wollstonecraft*, p. 9.

13. R. M. Janes, "On the Reception of Mary Wollstonecraft's *A Vindication of the Rights of Woman*", in *Journal of the History of Ideas*, Vol. 39, No. 2 (April–June 1978), pp. 293–294; see also Gary Kelly, *Revolutionary Feminism: The Mind and Career of Mary Wollstonecraft* (Basingstoke: Macmillan, 1992), pp. 168–170.

14. Janes, "On the Reception", pp. 296–297.

15. Mary Wollstonecraft, *Défense des droits des femmes; suivie de quelques considérations sur des sujets politiques et moraux* (Paris: Buisson; Lyon: Bruyset, 1792).

16. Taylor, *Mary Wollstonecraft*, p. 171.

17. See Kelly, *Revolutionary Feminism*, p. 165.

18. Mary Wollstonecraft, *A Historical and Moral View of the Origin and Progress of the French Revolution, and the Effect It Has Produced in Europe* [hereafter, *French Revolution*], Vol. 1 (London: J. Johnson, 1794), in *The Works of Mary Wollstonecraft*, ed. by Janet Todd and Marilyn Butler, Vol. 6 (London: William Pickering, 1989), p. 166. There was no volume 2. See also James Conniff, "Edmund Burke and His Critics: The Case of Mary Wollstonecraft", in *Journal of the History of Ideas*, Vol. 60, No. 2 (April 1999), p. 307.

19. Wollstonecraft, *French Revolution*, pp. 232–233.

20. See Kelly, *Revolutionary Feminism*, pp. 153–154, 160.

21. Wollstonecraft, *French Revolution*, p. 47.

22. *Ibid.*, p. 46.

23. *Ibid.*, p. 166.

24. See her *Letters Written During a Short Residence in Sweden, Norway, and Denmark* (London: Printed for J. Johnson, 1796).

This work was subsequently translated into Dutch, Portuguese, and German.

25. Tomalin, *The Life*, pp. 224, 234–235; and Wardle, *Mary Wollstonecraft*, pp. 244–246.
26. Mary Wollstonecraft, *A Vindication of the Rights of Men, in a Letter to the Right Honourable Edmund Burke; Occasioned by his Reflections on the Revolution in France* [hereafter, VRM], in Wollstonecraft, *Vindications* [Note 3], pp. 8, 7.
27. *Ibid.*, p. 16.
28. *Ibid.*, pp. 23–24.
29. *Ibid.*, pp. 13, 53.
30. *Ibid.*, pp. 20, 31, 33.
31. See *ibid.*, p. 9.
32. *Ibid.*, pp. 12–13.
33. Mary Poovey, *The Proper Lady and the Woman Writer: Ideology as Style in the Works of Mary Wollstonecraft, Mary Shelley, and Jane Austen* (Chicago: University of Chicago Press, 1984), p. 59.
34. Lena Halidenius, "The Primacy of Right: On the Triad of Liberty, Equality and Virtue in Wollstonecraft's Political Thought", in *British Journal for the History of Philosophy*, Vol. 15, No. 1 (2007), pp. 75–99.
35. As Helidenius has pointed out in *Ibid.*, pp. 77, 82.
36. Virgiinia Sapiro, *A Vindication of Political Virtue: The Political Theory of Mary Wollstonecraft* (Chicago: University of Chicago Press, 1992), p. 233.
37. VRM, p. 61.
38. Eileen M. Hunt, "The Family as Cave, Platoon and Prison: The Three Stages of Wollstonecraft's Philosophy of the Family", in *Review of Politics*, Vol. 64, No. 1 (Winter 2002), p. 84.
39. Moira Ferguson, "Mary Wollstonecraft and the Problematic of Slavery", in *Feminist Review*, No. 42 (Autumn 1992), p. 86.
40. Kelly, *Revolutionary Feminism*, p. 100.
41. See *Ibid.*, pp. 100–107.
42. Wardle, *Mary Wollstonecraft*, pp. 143–144.
43. *Ibid.*, p. 157.
44. *Ibid.*
45. Wollstonecraft, *A Vindication of the Rights of Woman: with Strictures on Political and Moral Subjects* [hereafter, VRW], in *Vindications* [Note 3], p. 82.

46. *Ibid.*, pp. 95, 78.
47. *Ibid.*, pp. 68–69.
48. *Ibid.*, pp. 87, 158.
49. Sapiro, *A Vindication of Political Virtue*, pp. 240, 244. Concerning her criticism of Rousseau, see also: Taylor, *Mary Wollstonecraft*, pp. 73–86; and Poovey, *The Proper Lady and the Woman Writer*, pp. 71–72.
50. VRW, p. 74.
51. Jean-Jacques Rousseau, *Emile*, trans. by B. Foxley (London: Dent, 1974), pp. 325, 370, as quoted in John Darling and Maaike Van De Pijpekamp, "Rousseau on the Education, Domination and Violation of Women", in *British Journal of Education*, Vol. 42, No. 2 (June 1994), p. 118.
52. Darling and Van De Pijpekamp, "Rousseau on the Education", p. 117.
53. Rousseau, as quoted in *ibid.*, p. 120.
54. Martina Reuter, "'Like a Fanciful Kind of Half Being': Mary Wollstonecraft's Criticism of Jean-Jacques Rousseau", in *Hypatia*, Vol. 29, No. 4 (Fall 2014), p. 928.
55. VRW, pp. 74, 76.
56. VRM, p. 48.
57. *Ibid.*, p. 22; and VRW, p. 99.
58. VRW, p. 114.
59. *Ibid.*, p. 117. See also the fair-minded discussion of *Vindication* in Kelly, *Revolutionary Feminism*, pp. 107–139.
60. Sapiro, *A Vindication of Political Virtue*, p. 225.
61. VRW, p. 119.
62. *Ibid.*, p. 108.
63. Wardle, *Mary Wollstonecraft*, p. 168.
64. Virginia Sapiro, "Wollstonecraft, Feminism, and Democracy: 'Being Bastilled'", in Maria J. Falco (ed.), *Feminist Interpretations of Mary Wollstonecraft* (University Park: The Pennsylvania State University Press, 1996), p. 33.
65. Wendy Gunther-Canada, "'The Same Subject Continued': Two Hundred Years of Wollstonecraft Scholarship", in Falco (ed.), *Feminist Interpretations*, pp. 213–214; and Kelly, *Revolutionary Feminism*, p. 225.
66. Eileen Hunt Botting and Christine Carey, "Wollstonecraft's Philosophical Impact on Nineteenth-Century American Women's

Rights", in *American Journal of Political Science*, Vol. 48, No. 4 (October 2004), pp. 707–722; confirmed in Penny A. Weiss, "Wollstonecraft and Rousseau: The Gendered Fate of Political Theorists", in Falco (ed.), *Feminist Interpretations*, p. 26.

67. Hunt, "The Family as Cave", p. 92.

68. *Ibid.*, p. 82; and Wardle, *Mary Wollstonecraft*, p. 152. Regarding Wollstonecraft's impact, see also Taylor, *Mary Wollstonecraft*, pp. 247–252.

CHAPTER 6

Conclusion: The Anglo-American Enlightenment in Historical Context

Sabrina P. Ramet

Abstract It was in reaction to the Thirty Years' War that Benedictus de Spinoza, Samuel von Pufendorf, and John Locke advocated religious toleration, linking this to Reason, Morality, individual rights, and liberty. By defending individual rights in the religious sphere and in conscience, they opened the gates to the European Enlightenment.

Keywords Reason · Morality · Liberty · Progress · Rights · God · Thirty Years' War

What was the Anglo-American Enlightenment all about anyway? There were four things which repeatedly received stress in the years of the Enlightenment, beginning with Spinoza and continuing with Locke, Jefferson, Madison, and, in Prussia, Kant. These were Reason, Morality, Liberty, Progress, and Rights, which were seen as *mutually entailed* and interactive. Enlightenment thinkers placed enormous faith in the power of human Reason. They held Morality to be closely related to Reason. John Locke, for example, argued that there exist natural (moral) laws and that they are "(1) discernible by the combined work of reason and sense experience, and (2) binding on human beings in virtue of being

S. P. Ramet and T. L. Knutsen, *Key Thinkers of the English, Scottish and American Enlightenments*,
https://doi.org/10.1007/978-3-031-62454-4_6

decreed by God."[1] Hume, as is known, offered an alternative approach, developing a "system of *secular* ethics."[2] Insofar as Reason, Morality, Liberty, Progress, and Rights are mutually entailed, one may say that *Liberty is a fundamental right*. Chapters 2, 4, and 5 stress especially the themes of Reason, Morality, Liberty, and Rights, while the Introduction and Chapter 3 also place stress on Progress.

Where Morality was concerned, Spinoza argued that to be moral was to be rational; indeed, Spinoza defined morality as "[t]he desire to do good, generated by our living according to *the guidance of reason*."[3] It followed, for him, that "acting from virtue is nothing but acting from the guidance of reason,"[4] and that "evil actions are the product of ignorance and impotence."[5] Kant's view similarly links reason and morality with his presentation of his Categorical Imperative "as an objective, *rationally necessary* and unconditional principle that we must follow."[6] For Kant, thus, there was no freedom to be immoral.

For Jefferson and Madison likewise it was impossible to embody one of these three factors (Reason, Morality, and Liberty) without embodying the other two. Although they differed about God, the major Enlightenment thinkers uniformly rejected the traditional teaching about an all-knowing, all-powerful, all-good God. The difficulty with this, as Hume pointed out, was that such a God would not, for example, have allowed as he put it in *The Natural History of Religion*, "The excessive drought of this season: The cold and rains of another" which would generally be understood as "evil," at least from most people's point of view.[7] What Hume concluded from his considerations of suffering caused by perturbations of nature was that God, if there is a God, could at best be described as "amoral."[8] It is obvious that people must have the possibility to commit evil deeds, and no one, to the best of my knowledge, has ever denied this (although Max Stirner, the infamous nihilist, denied that the word "evil" had any substantive meaning). But *all* the Enlightenment thinkers agreed that there is no merit in doing evil as such. And as already stated, Kant denied that one could be free without at the same time striving to behave in a moral way. Or, as Spinoza put it, someone who craves immoral things or wants to behave in an immoral way, is a slave to his (or her) cravings and, thus, not a free person.[9] A truly free person, Kant and Spinoza argued, strives to behave in a moral way, and both Jefferson and Madison read the works of Spinoza with high interest, as already mentioned in Chapter 4.

Nonetheless, the Enlightenment thinkers offered quite varied accounts of God. Spinoza's account, equating God with Nature, was obscure enough that he was repeatedly accused of being a pantheist—a charge he vehemently denied. Paine critiqued and mocked the Christian Bible, rejected the Christian creed, and subscribed to a version of Deism. Jefferson and Madison were members of the Anglican/Episcopalian Church but also Deists. Kant was a nonbeliever who argued, as other Enlightenment figures (such as Hume) did, that the moral law had a value in and of itself and was binding without requiring endorsement by an omniscient God but felt, nonetheless, that ordinary people, who could not understand the reason for behaving morally without the threat of hellfire, should be taught to believe Christian teachings.[10] And Locke was a latitudinarian who felt that there was little basis for choosing among the sundry sects. On balance, then, the Anglo-American Enlightenment fostered secularism, thereby placing reason as the arbiter of issues which had earlier been referred to religious faith and doctrine.

It was in reaction to the Thirty Years' War (1618–1648), a war fueled by interreligious animosity and competition,[11] that John Locke, Benedictus de Spinoza, and Samuel von Pufendorf—all, coincidentally, born in 1632—protested against religious hegemonism and pleaded for religious toleration.[12] Their works include: Locke's *Essay on Toleration* (1667), *A Letter concerning Toleration* (1689), *A Second Letter concerning Toleration* (1690), and *Two Treatises on Government* (1690); Spinoza's *Tractatus Theologico-Politicus* of 1670 and his *Ethics*, published only after his death in 1677; and Pufendorft's *De statu imperii germanici liber unus* (1667), *De jure naturae et gentium* (1672), and *De habitu religionis Christianae ad vitam civilem* (1698).

The first great book of the Enlightenment, thus, was Spinoza's *Tractatus Theologico-Politicus*; the last great book of the Enlightenment was Kant's *The Metaphysics of Morals* of 1797; the most often read book of the Enlightenment today is surely Locke's *Second Treatise of Government* (1690), although his (first) *Letter Concerning Toleration* continues to enjoy a wide readership. The most cited work of the American Enlightenment might be Madison's *Memorial and Remonstrance against Religious Assessments* (1785), in which its author protested against the initiative in Virginia to exact taxes to support the Anglican Church.

According to Maurice Cranston, who wrote a classic biography of the English thinker,[13] John Locke's central concern was liberty[14] although summarizing any thinker with just one word risks oversimplification and provoking objections from those who might think that Locke's central concern was, perhaps, something else. According to Julius Steinberg, a professor at Brooklyn College, Spinoza's "chief concern…is with human liberation."[15] For Kant, the Categorical Imperative loomed large. Still others may wish to reduce the Enlightenment as a whole to merely Rights and perhaps subsume everything else, even Kant's Categorical Imperative, under that rubric or perhaps argue that the Enlightenment was allegedly about "bourgeois" rights, offering little if anything to the working class. Where the Americans are concerned, "liberty" was on the lips of all three of the thinkers we have discussed and what seems clear in all the preceding chapters is that all of the thinkers we have discussed had some interest in defending individual rights. Here it is worth mentioning the American *Declaration of Independence* (1776), written mainly by Thomas Jefferson, and *The Rights of Man, Part One* (1791) and *The Rights of Man, Part Two* (1792), both written by Thomas Paine.

The Enlightenment undermined traditional monarchy (associated with the claim to a divine right of kings), promoted enlightened monarchy (best exemplified in the reigns of Maria Theresa (Empress Consort of the Holy Roman Empire, 1740–1780) and Joseph II (Holy Roman Emperor, 1765–1790), and spawned revolution—first in America (1776), shortly thereafter in France (1789), and finally across much of Europe in 1848. It conjured notions of democracy, promoted religious toleration, and, as suggested above, provided a powerful defense of individualism.

Although the classic era of the Enlightenment may be said to have come to an end in the course of the French Revolutionary Wars which broke out at the end of the eighteenth century, the legacy of that era influenced both nineteenth-century thinkers such as Georg Wilhelm Friedrich Hegel and twentieth-century philosophers such as John Rawls. The Enlightenment was one of the great watersheds in history, with lasting impact and having continuing importance.

NOTES

1. "Locke: Ethics", in *Internet Encyclopedia of Philosophy*, at https://iep.utm.edu/locke-et/#:~:text=The%20main%20lines%20of%20Locke's,of%20being%20decreed%20by%20God [accessed on 13 January 2024], p. 10 of 22 (my emphasis).

2. "Hume on Religion", in *Stanford Encyclopedia of Philosophy*, at https://plato.stanford.edu/entries/hume-religion/, First published 4 October 2005; substantive revision 27 March 2017, copyright © 2017 by Paul Russell, at https://plato.stanford.edu/entries/hume-religion/ [accessed on 13 January 2024], p. 20 of 29 (my emphasis).
3. Benedictus de Spinoza, *Ethics*, trans. from Latin by Edwin Curley (London: Penguin Books, 1996), p. 134, comma added (my emphasis).
4. Ibid., p. 144.
5. Jusin Steinberg, Review of Matthew J. Kisner, *Spinoza on Human Freedom: Reason, Autonomy and the Good Life* (Cambridge: Cambridge University Press, 2016), in *Notre Dame Philosophical Review*, https://ndpr.nd.edu/reviews/spinoza-on-human-freedom-reason-autonomy-and-the-good-life/ [accessed on 13 January 2024], p. 6 of 8.
6. "Kant's Moral Philosophy", in *Stanford Encyclopedia of Philosophy*, First published 23 February 2024; substantive revision 21 January 2022, copyright © 2022 by Robert Johnson and Adam Cureton, at https://plato.stanford.edu/entries/kant-moral/ [accessed on 13 January 2024], p. 1 of 25.
7. As quoted in James Tarrant, "Hume's Fundamental Problem of Evil", in *Philosophy*, Vol. 89, No. 350 (October 2014), p. 610.
8. Ibid., p. 620.
9. See Spinoza, *Ethics*, passim.
10. See Sabrina P. Ramet, "Kant on Ethics and Politics", in *Eastern Review*, Vol. 8 (2019), pp. 183–199.
11. See Peter H. Wilson, "The Causes of the Thirty Years War (1618–1648)", in *The English Historical Review*, Vol. 123, No. 502 (2008), pp. 554–586.
12. See my article, "Spinoza, Liberalism and 'the Class of 1632'", in *Teorija in Praksa*, Vol. 60, No. 2 (2023), pp. 295–315.
13. Maurice Cranston, *Locke: A Biography* (London: Longmans, 1959).
14. Maurice Cranston, "Locke and Liberty", in *The Wilson Quarterly*, Vol. 10, No. 5 (Winter 1986), p. 82.
15. Steinberg, Review, p. 1 of 8.

INDEX OF NAMES

© The Editor(s) (if applicable) and The Author(s), under exclusive license to Springer Nature Switzerland AG 2024
S. P. Ramet and T. L. Knutsen, *Key Thinkers of the English, Scottish and American Enlightenments,*
https://doi.org/10.1007/978-3-031-62454-4

Index of Subjects

GPSR Compliance

The European Union's (EU) General Product Safety Regulation (GPSR) is a set of rules that requires consumer products to be safe and our obligations to ensure this.

If you have any concerns about our products, you can contact us on ProductSafety@springernature.com

In case Publisher is established outside the EU, the EU authorized representative is:

Springer Nature Customer Service Center GmbH
Europaplatz 3
69115 Heidelberg, Germany

The manufacturer's authorised representative in the EU is Springer
Nature Customer Service Centre GmbH, Europaplatz 3, 69115 Heidelberg,
Germany. If you have any concerns regarding our products, please
contact ProductSafety@springernature.com

Printed and bound by CPI Group (UK) Ltd, Croydon, CR0 4YY
29/04/2026
02099531-0007